# The
# Patient
## in the
# White
# Coat

# The
# Patient
## in the
# White
# Coat

## My Odyssey from Health to Illness and Back

### Rosalind Kaplan, MD

PUBLISHING

New York

© 2010 Rosalind Kaplan, MD

Published by Kaplan Publishing, a division of Kaplan, Inc.
1 Liberty Plaza, 24th Floor
New York, NY 10006

Printed in the United States of America

10  9  8  7  6  5  4  3  2  1

ISBN: 978-1-60714-694-0

**Library of Congress Cataloging-in-Publication Data**

Kaplan, Rosalind.
    The patient in the white coat : my notes on illness, healing, and surviving a chronic disease / by Rosalind Kaplan.
        p. ; cm.
    ISBN 978-1-60714-694-0
    1. Kaplan, Rosalind—Health. 2. Hepatitis C—Patients—Pennsylvania—Biography. 3. Physicians—Pennsylvania—Biography. I. Title.
    [DNLM: 1. Physician's Role—United States—Personal Narratives. 2. Physicians, Women—United States—Personal Narratives. 3. Chronic Disease—psychology—United States—Personal Narratives. 4. Hepatitis C—psychology—United States—Personal Narratives. 5. Sick Role—United States—Personal Narratives. W 62 K17p 2010]
    RC848.H425K37 2010
    616.3'62300922—dc22

2010010702

*In memory of my father, James Barsky,*

*who taught me about books, science,*

*and unconditional love.*

*"Illness is the nightside of life, a more onerous citizenship.*

*Everyone who is born holds dual citizenship,*

*in the kingdom of the well and in the kingdom of the sick."*

—SUSAN SONTAG,
*ILLNESS AS METAPHOR*

# CONTENTS

CHAPTER 1

# The Diagnosis

M Y CHART SAT in the plastic bin mounted on the outside of the door to the examination room. Inside the room, a generic cubicle with a shiny tile floor, harsh fluorescent lights, and the requisite single chair, I sat, anxiously awaiting Dr. Goodman's arrival. The door was ajar, and I could see out into the hallway, which was silent and empty. The deep-blue carpet reflected the cool calm that everyone I'd seen that day seemed to possess, but that I was sorely lacking.

I felt a wave of nausea for the hundredth time that afternoon. I tapped my foot and leafed through another dog-eared, outdated copy of *Ladies' Home Journal*.

I glanced up at my chart. Some answers had to be in there. I'd come to Dr. Goodman, a specialist in gastrointestinal diseases, several weeks earlier because of some abnormal blood test results, specifically tests indicating that my liver was inflamed. My first visit with Dr. Goodman led only to more blood tests, and now this follow-up appointment was to review the results.

I had a bad feeling. An educated guess, I suppose, backed by four years at the University of Pennsylvania School of Medicine, three years in an academic internal medicine residency, and about eight months as an assistant professor in General Internal Medicine in a university hospital. I was not a seasoned practitioner, but the experience I had was high quality. I hadn't graduated first in my class, nor had I memorized Harrison's *Principles of Internal Medicine,* the classic medicine text, from cover to cover like some of my colleagues, but I'd developed a reputation in my residency for having keen intuition. It was this intuition that was making me so nervous now.

I cursed myself once again for ordering the original blood tests. It's one of the double-edged swords of being a doctor. We can order our own blood tests and X-rays and medications. That doesn't mean we should. Who was it who said, "It's a fool who would have himself for a patient"?

My decision to order my own tests happened about six months after I finished my residency, and about three months before this visit with Dr. Goodman, when my mother died unexpectedly. She'd been fine, healthy but for some mild high blood pressure, until Christmas Eve, 1990, when, according to my father, she awoke in the morning, turned to him, and said, "Call 911, I'm dying." And then she did.

We never found out the cause of her death. My father, raised an Orthodox Jew, didn't want an autopsy, and my brother and I respected his wishes, though it would have given us comfort to know. It wasn't until weeks later, after we had exhausted all the tears and guilt and agonizing over whether her death could have been prevented or foreseen, that we realized we had lost more than the opportunity for closure. We had also lost part of our family medical history, and the ability to assess our own risks.

"Well, it must have been a heart attack like it said on the death certificate," Bob said, as we went over the events for perhaps the 30th time.

"No, I still think it was a ruptured aneurysm in her brain," I told him. "Nobody in her family ever had heart disease, and she didn't have any risk factors except her blood pressure. Dad specifically told me she wasn't clutching at her chest. The whole thing sounds more neurologic."

"We're never going to know. So we should both get physicals and have everything checked that could have anything to do with either of those things. What tests should we be getting?"

"Well," I said, "some aneurysms are congenital, like berry aneurysms, so you should ask your doctor for an MRI and MRA of your brain, just to make sure. For heart, it's blood pressure and cholesterol, and you'd better start exercising."

We made a pact to get the necessary tests done.

My brother, who is an economist, went to his doctor and got the tests done. I called a neurologist about the brain studies, but the cholesterol tests seemed routine enough to order for myself. So I went to the employee health office at the hospital where I worked. I filled out the blood slip listing myself as the patient and as the ordering physician. And when I was checking off which tests to do, I thought, *well, why not just do the whole routine battery of tests?* I ordered a blood count and liver function tests and thyroid and electrolytes along with the cholesterol.

I didn't believe in being my own doctor. I'd seen friends in my medicine residency do it quite often and saw the potential for trouble. My friend Lori, for instance, had terrible asthma. The stress of 36-hour shifts and sleep deprivation, along with the dusty, moldy on-call room, set off attacks that would have sent anyone else to the emergency room. Instead she medicated herself, gave herself oxygen, and kept working. She periodically ended up hospitalized when her asthma became uncontrollable, and I can't help but believe she would have done better if she'd been following the orders of an asthma specialist. Other residents ordered their own chest X-rays when they suspected they had pneumonia, or asked a friend for an antibiotic prescription, or simply took samples of medicine for their symptoms from the closet in the outpatient clinic. All well and good if they got better, but if they didn't, or had an allergic reaction to the medication or some other complication, solving the problem became much more difficult later.

There were obvious reasons why the interns and residents took medical short-cuts. Time was the one you'd hear about if you asked. We started work at 7 A.M. and worked until at least 6 P.M., and every third or fourth night, worked through the night. Nobody asked for time off for illness unless it was dire; that was the macho culture we worked in. Of course, we were working in a hospital and had plenty of excellent doctors we could have consulted right there. But asking for medical help from our superiors was an admission of weakness, the breaking of a tacit rule. No one ever told us to act as though, as doctors, we were not ourselves flesh and blood, vulnerable to the same malfunctions and maladies as our patients. And yet we learned the behavior, the beginning of setting ourselves apart, of disbelieving our mortality so as to tolerate the mortality of others.

Ordering my own tests did seem innocent enough at the time, but I was descending the slippery slope. Even ordering tests for myself had significant ramifications, because tests have results, and if the results indicated that something required further investigation or treatment, I would have to make decisions. And emotions would creep in, and an uncontrolled chain of events might ensue. And while I knew something like that could happen, I just didn't think it would. The tests were, after all, just routine.

The technician labeled four tubes with my name, then put the tourniquet on my arm and wiped it with alcohol. She filled the tubes with blood. I left and didn't think about it again until the report appeared on my desk four days later.

I got to work as usual that morning, checked my schedule (patient hours, student lecture, general medicine section meeting, clinic hours), and then began to sort through the papers on my desk. My labs were mixed in with the lab reports on some of my patients, so I signed off on several pages of patient labs before finding my own blood results. I looked down the neat column of numbers, with the normal lab values listed on the right side. The first page had my blood counts, sodium, potassium, kidney function, and a normal cholesterol profile, so I was feeling triumphant, until I turned the page and saw the numbers listed as "out of range"—my liver enzymes, known as the ALT and AST. High values generally indicate some kind of inflammation of the liver. Mine were between two and three times the normal values, considered mildly to moderately elevated but giving no clue as to the cause.

I stared at the page. Surely this was some kind of mistake.

I had no history of liver problems, and liver tests checked in the past had been normal.... No, not a mistake, I'd watched the technician label the tubes and draw the blood... so what was this?

I needed to think rationally, clinically. Causes of liver inflammation. Most common were viruses—specifically hepatitis viruses, which could be serious, but also other minor, transient viral illnesses—and toxins (alcohol and medications). There were other causes, other diseases causing liver problems, but they were much less likely in a young, healthy person. The term *hepatitis* actually means simply inflammation of the liver, although now when we say just the word *hepatitis,* we generally are referring to one of the specific viruses that attack the liver, hepatitis A, B, and C (hepatitis D and E viruses have been isolated, but we come across them much more rarely). Other things that inflame the liver are usually referred to more specifically, such as alcoholic hepatitis or autoimmune hepatitis.

Like the stoic, stubborn doctor I was, I decided to try to solve the problem myself. I didn't even tell my husband, Larry, right away. He was under some work-related stress at the time, trying to prove himself as junior faculty in the same general medicine section where I worked. He'd been there a year longer than I and was serious about a career in academic general medicine, whereas I was just starting out and was not yet sure of my career path. Larry was under pressure to start a clinical research project and to build a clinical practice. He had recently taken a significant amount of personal time off, first when our son was born six months earlier, then two months prior when my mother died. I didn't want to place another burden on him unnecessarily.

So when I saw the abnormal liver tests, I eliminated all potential liver toxins from my system—alcohol, Tylenol, and the antidepressant medication I'd been on since my mother died—and rechecked the blood tests after three weeks. Still abnormal. I started to feel anxious. Even a little panicked—I truly had no idea what it all meant yet, but it couldn't be good. Ongoing abnormal liver function tests in the absence of toxins implied some kind of chronic process.

When the liver is acutely inflamed because of a short-lived virus or toxin exposure, cells die but regenerate, and there is usually complete recovery, generally over days or weeks. But when the inflammation goes on for longer periods of time, the liver can become permanently damaged. Since the liver is an organ with many very important functions, including metabolism of the majority of foods and drugs that we ingest, manufacture of bile to emulsify the proteins we eat, and synthesis of glucose from its building blocks when our blood sugar becomes low, a healthy liver is extremely important.

I curbside-consulted every expert I knew without letting on that it was about me. I was hoping for some brilliant revelation, but all I got were the obvious answers, what I already knew—toxins, viral, could be almost anything; the patient needs this further test and that further test and should be referred to a specialist. It was time to tell Larry.

"Abnormal liver function tests don't necessarily mean anything," Larry said flatly.

"They mean *something*. They were normal a year or so ago and now they're not, so something's wrong. We just don't know what."

"I'm sure it's nothing. You should just go see a gastroenter-ologist and get the workup done. It'll be fine." Larry turned back to the journal he was reading.

I stood in the kitchen, holding our son, Max, and feeling a combination of irritated and lonely.

In all fairness, Larry's apparent nonchalance was more likely denial than lack of caring. He wanted so badly for me to be fine that he couldn't imagine any other outcome, but I didn't understand that then.

I would have liked it if Larry had offered to go with me for further tests, but it looked like I was on my own. I could have told him I needed him to come, but I didn't. Because I'd started to doubt my intuition. If he turned out to be right, and I was fine, then I would feel guilty about having bothered him. I'd go get my tests, and then we'd all go happily on with our lives. On the other hand, if I was right, I could be justifiably angry at him later for ignoring my needs, and we all like to have a little justi-fiable anger, don't we?

I chose Dr. Goodman as my gastroenterologist (a doctor spe-cializing in the digestive tract, including the liver and gallblad-der) because he was not at my own hospital, and I knew him from a previous GI problem I'd had. He was both well respected and kind. He was connected to a major medical center in case I needed a "super-specialist" in liver disease.

Here in Dr. Goodman's exam room, I was growing impatient. He was running quite late. I'd run out of magazines—not that I could really concentrate, but there weren't even any pictures to look at now. I started pacing around the room. I was cold, also, even though the day was fairly warm for early April and I was sure there was no air conditioning on in the room. My eyes darted back to the chart.

What the hell? Why couldn't I just look at it? It was *my* chart. A lot of people don't understand that, but the chart belongs to the patient, really, and I had every right to see what was in it....

I glanced into the hallway. Still empty. Still silent. I grabbed the chart out of the plastic bin on the door and closed the door a bit more so it was just very slightly ajar.

I sat down at the doctor's desk area and began to read the sparse recent notes and labs.

Dr. Goodman's first entry, on the 12th of March, noted the high levels of ALT and AST, the major liver enzymes, from the tests results I gave him, and he wrote to check for viral and autoimmune diseases.

The next pages were the lab results. The ALT and AST were still high—a little better, but not normal; I didn't have hepatitis A or B, and I had immunity to hepatitis B from the series of vaccines given at the beginning of medical school. But the next line read:

Hep C Ab Positive
*What?* I read the line again.
Hep C Ab Positive
*I think that means I have hepatitis C…*

*Don't panic. Think.* I needed to gather up what I knew about hepatitis C. Usually I can collect the information about a diagnosis in little packets from my brain: the pages from the textbook, the slides from a med school lecture, the clinical pearls offered during a case presentation, the practical experience from a patient I'd treated. But this time it unfolded as a horror movie playing in my head:

The last year of my residency. A young light-skinned black man lying in the ICU. His skin was jaundiced, the color of mustard, his eyes an almost fluorescent yellow. Spindly extremities protruded from his grotesquely swollen belly. He was 28, in the end stages of liver failure, waiting for a liver transplant. He got the disease from shooting drugs with dirty needles. When I took care of him in the hospital, researchers had just isolated the hepatitis C virus. In the ICU, he opened his mouth, and blood spewed out violently, splattering the walls and ceiling. He had a condition called esophageal varices—his liver was so scarred that the blood couldn't circulate through it. It backed up into the veins in his esophagus. The veins dilated and finally ruptured. The only way to stop the bleeding was to blow up a balloon device in the man's esophagus to apply pressure to the veins. He lived through this bleed but didn't make it to the transplant.

I remembered thinking what a horrible disease this was, and how awful it would be to have it. I also remembered thinking what a silly thought that was. Yes, it was a terrible disease, but one I would never get. One I would never get…

*What am I doing with this disease? Where did I get it? From whom? It's contracted from contact with infected blood…I'd had no transfusions, don't shoot drugs; sex? Doubt it…Oh, God, what about my son—could I have given this to him?*

Just then Dr. Goodman pushed the door open and walked in.

"Just like a doctor, to be reading your own chart," he chided me in his booming voice.

I looked up, shell-shocked.

"What's the matter?" Clearly this was new information for him as well as for me.

"Well, look."

He picked up the chart and looked through the labs.

"Oh, you've got hep C," he said, offhandedly, as though he were telling me I had brown hair. "That makes sense. Slightly high, fluctuating liver function tests, and you're at risk because you're a healthcare worker."

"But that's a bad diagnosis to have!"

"No, not necessarily. Probably a lot of people have it. Think of all the people you see with mildly abnormal liver function tests who just get watched for years. They might have it; we don't know yet. You need to go see one of the two people at U. Penn who are doing the research and starting to treat people. They'll tell you what to do."

He had a point. There were people who supposedly had this disease and never developed any symptoms. But there were also people like my jaundiced patient with the esophageal bleeding. And hepatitis C was known to be chronic and incurable, from what I had learned.

"You're talking about the interferon studies?" I asked. *Interferon* was a word I'd heard tossed about once or twice in relation to chronic hepatitis. I knew almost nothing about it, except that it was a purely experimental drug.

"Yes, but as I said, you need to talk to these guys at Penn."

I knew there was nothing more that Dr. Goodman could tell me. He didn't have a crystal ball. If I had pushed him, he'd likely have reassured me that I wasn't going to end up in liver failure, but it wouldn't make me feel better; I probably wouldn't have believed him. I took the information he offered me, thanked him, and left.

I never really knew what the phrase "don't know whether you're coming or going" meant until that day. In the space of minutes, I wavered a hundred times between believing that I would die an awful death from liver disease and that I would be just fine. I didn't have enough information to judge, but I would soon find out that the information wasn't forthcoming anyway.

When I left Dr. Goodman's office, I called my husband and told him the diagnosis. I know I was calm, and when he asked if I was okay I told him I was. He stayed in his denial state and took me at my word.

"Well, you'll see the people at Penn, and if necessary, you'll get treated. It's going to be fine. We'll talk when you get home," he told me. I forgot that I wanted to be angry at him. We had a baby to take care of. Somebody was going to have to stay calm no matter what.

As I walked to the parking garage, I wondered why I didn't want to cry. Plenty of time for that later, I reasoned. I got into my dark-red Subaru station wagon. On the passenger seat lay my starched white doctor's coat, stethoscope in the pocket, hospital ID tag clipped to the lapel. I tossed it into the back, with the baby seat, a remnant of another life.

# CHAPTER 2

# You Need to Know a Little Something

*Hepatos*—deriving from the Greek, meaning, of course, "liver."

*itis*—suffix deriving from the modern Latin, meaning "inflammation."

Thus, the word *hepatitis,* "inflammation of the liver."

'D NEVER STUDIED Latin or Greek, only French. "Medicalese," the made-up name for language doctors use and patients often can't understand, is full of words closely tied to Latin and/or Greek, yet I never felt at a disadvantage. In the modern world of medicine, it is Spanish, for the purpose of communicating with patients, that really would have been useful. Still, as I struggle to explain hepatitis to my readers, I find myself reaching for Latin derivatives, trying to go back to the root of the problem.

Inflammation of the liver. There are many different causes of liver inflammation, and the types of hepatitis are generally named for their causes. Liver inflammation can be caused by toxins, such as alcohol or drugs ("alcoholic hepatitis" or "toxic hepatitis"), or by an overactive immune system, in which the body attacks its own tissues ("autoimmune hepatitis"). Still, the sort of hepatitis most commonly discussed is viral hepatitis, and that, too, is divided into several different types, one of which is our subject here, hepatitis C.

The alphabet soup of hepatitis viruses is confusing to many people. The most common viruses causing hepatitis are A, B, and C. They all cause liver inflammation, but there are important differences among them.

Hepatitis A is carried through contaminated food and water, and spread by poor hygiene (the "oral-fecal" route). It can make its victims very sick, with fevers, nausea, vomiting, jaundice, abdominal pain, and fatigue. In rare cases, it even causes liver failure, which can lead to death. However, it generally runs its course and the patient recovers completely with just supportive care such as rest and fluids (it is "self-limited"). Once it resolves, the patient is immune, and so cannot be reinfected. There is a vaccine for hepatitis A, currently recommended for children and for travelers to many foreign countries.

Hepatitis B is carried via blood and body fluids, and spread primarily now by needle-sharing in drug abuse and by sex. Blood transfusions were a source before blood was routinely screened. Most hepatitis B infections are self-limited, but, like hepatitis A, can make a patient quite ill. Unlike those with hepatitis A, though, a small percentage of hepatitis B patients develop a chronic state of infection or a chronic carrier state. In the chronically infected state, the patient has ongoing liver inflammation and remains infectious (similarly, as we'll see, to hepatitis C). The chronic inflammation can eventually lead to abnormal cell growth and liver cancer called hepatocellular carcinoma. In the carrier state, the patient recovers completely but can infect others for an indefinite period of time. Before hepatitis C came along, hepatitis B was the liver disease that liver specialists struggled with most and that generated the most research interest. However, most patients infected with hepatitis B clear the virus and become immune. There is an effective vaccine against hepatitis B, given to all babies, adolescents, and healthcare workers, as well as to some travelers and other susceptible people.

If hepatitis B seems baffling, hepatitis C is even more of a conundrum. Until 1990, viral hepatitis that was not caused by hepatitis A or B was simply referred to as non-A, non-B hepatitis. Then the hepatitis C virus was isolated, and it became clear that many, if not most, of the cases of abnormal liver function tests with no identifiable cause were actually due to hep C. The virus is blood-borne, spread in the same way as hepatitis B but not as efficiently. It is much more difficult to contract hep C, say, through a needle stick with a small drop of blood or through a sexual contact, than it is to contract hep B. That is not to say that those methods of viral spread do not occur. However, most cases of hep C were contracted from blood transfusions before 1992, when routine testing of the blood supply began, or are the result of needle-sharing by IV drug users both before and after 1992.

Hepatitis C remains puzzling to researchers in terms of the immune response. Most people who contract hepatitis C develop antibodies to it but do not become immune to it. In fact, 75 percent of patients who contract it never clear the virus from their bodies. Even more disconcerting is that most of the patients who get hepatitis C never know that they have it unless they are tested. They don't become acutely ill the way patients with hep A and B do. But some do, and it seems that it is those who become sickest who are most likely to clear the virus from their bodies. There is no available vaccine, and so far none on the horizon, since evoking an appropriate immune response remains elusive.

If people with hepatitis C don't usually get acutely ill, then what does happen to them? The patient may have no discernible symptoms at all, or may have subtle, nonspecific symptoms such as fatigue, malaise, achy joints, low-grade fevers, or even depression. Since the patient is unaware of the infection, and the infection becomes chronic, the symptoms may be ignored or attributed to such things as lack of sleep or other lifestyle issues. If the infection is diagnosed, it is usually because the patient's liver function is tested for routine reasons, or because the patient undergoes routine screening for hep C.

I don't want to be macabre or unnecessarily dramatic, but there are some facts about hep C that I found particularly disturbing, and it took me a while to absorb them. One is that hep C causes devastating disease in some people and no symptoms at all in others. The hep C virus is, in fact, the most common reason for liver transplant in the United States, and the most common cause of chronic liver disease and liver cancer in the Western world. My jaundiced, blood-vomiting patient was one of the unlucky, devastating cases. Nevertheless, the vast majority of hep C patients live for many years with minimal symptoms. The big problem is that despite an outward appearance of good health, these seemingly more fortunate patients have ongoing liver inflammation.

Let's think about what happens to the liver in this process. With prolonged inflammation, some of the liver cells die. Because we have so many liver cells, the liver is able to keep performing its functions, metabolizing toxins and synthesizing nutritional building blocks. Cells regenerate, at first in a regular, orderly way, keeping the normal architecture of the liver intact, at least in the beginning.

After years of chronic inflammation, the neat, interlocking filigree of liver cells begins to be replaced with fibrous tissue. Cell regeneration occurs, but not in the same ordered way, and it slows. Islands of cells begin to be isolated from one another and finally disappear in a sea of scar tissue. When the liver tissue becomes replaced by scar tissue, the organ is considered cirrhotic. It can no longer perform its functions. The remaining cells are at risk for dividing in a chaotic frenzy, becoming a liver cancer (hepatocellular carcinoma, or HCC, as in chronic hepatitis B), which occurs at a rate of about 1 to 4 percent once there is cirrhosis.

An estimated 20 to 30 percent of chronic hepatitis C cases will eventually lead to severe liver damage if not treated, and those patients will develop cirrhosis, liver failure, and possibly liver cancer. The good news is that the majority of hepatitis C sufferers—the other 70 to 80 percent—will not develop serious disease. Even if there is chronic inflammation, it does not mean it will progress to cirrhosis. Still, these patients may suffer symptoms, such as fatigue, malaise, depression, and body pain, as well as experience worry and stigma over having the disease. The problem is that there is really no way to know whether the disease will progress to cause serious damage or not.

To complicate the situation further, not everyone benefits equally from treatment. There are subtypes (known as sero-types) of the virus, and some are more sensitive to antiviral treatment than others. There are also other factors, such as age, sex, and viral load (the amount of virus in the bloodstream), that can predict response to treatment, but these predictions are not hard-and-fast rules. Some patients don't respond to treatment at all, others go into remission only to relapse, while still others reap the benefit of a long-term remission. There is no reliable way to predict who will tolerate treatment well and who will have lasting benefit, just as there is no reliable way to know who will have a good outcome without treatment.

By avoiding alcohol and other liver toxins, such as large amounts of Tylenol, and certain herbal and prescription as well as recreational drugs, those with hepatitis C can prevent further damage to their livers. Vaccination against hepatitis A and B, if the patient is not already immune, is advisable, so collaboration with the physician is essential to improve prognosis.

The number of new cases of hepatitis C dropped dramatically after testing of donated blood became routine in 1992, though there are still plenty of new cases—mostly in IV drug users who share needles. Since the majority of people infected aren't aware that they are infected, they unknowingly pass along their disease. Even though fewer people are getting infected now, hepatitis C will actually cause more sickness and death in the next two decades than ever before. This is because the larger number of cases infected before 1992 have now had the disease for more than 20 years, and the prolonged liver damage will be causing cirrhosis and liver failure in more of those patients.

It's estimated that 4,000,000 Americans are infected with the hepatitis C virus. While it may reek of sensationalism, with numbers like that—and most of those people unaware of their infections—it is no wonder that the media has referred to hep C as the "new epidemic," the "silent killer," and the "stealth virus."

Testing and treatment have improved since my ordeal, but at the time, the only widely available test for hep C was a blood test for antibody to the virus. That's the test that alerted Dr. Goodman to my infection. It is sensitive, but not specific (that is, it will find most cases of hep C but it will also be positive in some people who do not actually have chronic hep C). Combined with my abnormal liver function tests, it was pretty convincing evidence that I had hep C. Later, my blood was sent out to a research laboratory to test for presence of the virus itself, a much more specific test for ongoing infection. Now that test, a PCR test, is widely available and can be used to screen high-risk patients. Still, most people who are diagnosed find out they have the disease the way I did: accidentally, as a result of getting blood drawn for other reasons. Back in 1990, I was the tip of a huge iceberg. Most of that iceberg is still underwater.

Despite advances in testing and improvements in treatment since I was diagnosed, hepatitis C remains a diagnosis of tremendous uncertainty. That's the hardest part for most patients. I know it was for me. As I prepared to visit the liver specialist, it seemed as though the more I knew, the more questions the knowledge raised. It was clear that no one had the answers I really wanted.

# CHAPTER 3

# In the Kingdom
# of the Specialist

GASTROENTEROLOGY AND *Liver Diseases*, announced a large sign as Larry and I stepped off the elevator in one of the Hospital of the University of Pennsylvania's large, modern buildings. This was the place. "Yes, I do have a liver disease!" I felt like shouting, as we walked in the door to the suite. We found ourselves in a vast waiting room carpeted in mauve and filled with dark-wood chairs, upholstered in a mauve-tone pattern. It was the waiting-room style of the 1990s. The mauve was supposed to be calming. It didn't do the trick for me.

It had taken only a moment for me to get the picture that I had no power at all when I called to make the appointment with Dr. Payne. First, I got a recording that said, "You have reached the Division of Gastroenterology and Liver Diseases at the University of Pennsylvania. Please listen to all of the following choices before making your selection. If this is an emergency or you are a doctor or hospital calling for a consult, please press 1…" Well, this time, I couldn't press 1. I thought to myself, *I always press 1! But that's what I do when I'm a doctor calling another doctor about a patient. I can't do that now*…So I kept listening… "If you'd like to make an appointment, press 2." *Okay, then, that's what I want.* So I pressed 2. And it rang, and then another recording came on.

*Wait a minute!* I thought. *When you press 1, a person comes on right away! So what is this, when you press 2, you're not important anymore?* Right. So the second recording said, "If you want to make an appointment with Dr. Jones, press 1; with Dr. Smith, press 2," and so on, until it said Dr. Payne. Then I pressed the number. And it rang. And rang. And rang. Finally, after six rings, I got a recording: "This is Amanda Martin, secretary to Dr. Payne. I'm not at my desk right now. Please leave a message, and I will call you back at my earliest convenience." At *her* earliest convenience…

*Aaargh!!!* I considered calling back and pressing 1, but I knew it wasn't a good idea. Sure, I could have pulled rank and used my doctor status, but that wasn't a good idea either. I didn't want to get on anyone's bad side. Even irritating the secretary could have consequences. If she thought I was behaving in an entitled manner or being difficult, she might say something to the doctor, and he might begin with a preconceived notion about me. I needed this doctor on my side. No, I would go through proper channels. I'd be a patient, not a doctor.

I didn't have much personal experience with this yet from the doctor's side, as I had been out of training for only a few months. But I'd watched it with the older doctors I'd worked with, and I regret to say that now, years into practice, I feel somewhat ambivalent when a new patient, not yet part of my practice, pulls strings to get my attention. I think the reason is that I feel pressured to provide some special care or feel that I may not live up to the patient's expectations. This may not be correct, but it still creates an uncomfortable dynamic.

So I left a message, with my home and work phone numbers. And Amanda Martin didn't call me back that day. Or the next. So I called again, and left another message. Finally, she called back and offered me an appointment a month away, at a time that was in the middle of a workday for me. I asked her if there might be a later time.

"Oh, no," she replied, "we're squeezing you in as it is. It's this appointment or I'll have to put you on a waiting list."

I had a bit of a hard time believing this, but who was I to question? A month by today's standards may not seem a long wait, but it seemed like a lifetime away, and I wasn't about to make that wait any longer. I canceled my afternoon patients that day and asked Larry to do the same.

So here we were, in Dr. Payne's mauve waiting room at 2:30 P.M. I checked in with the receptionist and began filling out the new-patient forms. My appointment was at 3:00, but I needn't have worried about arriving early to complete the paperwork. Three o'clock came and went, as did 3:30 and 4:00, as we sat in the mauve waiting room. Larry read his *New England Journal of Medicine* and *Annals of Internal Medicine*. Too nervous to focus, I flipped through the typical waiting-room magazines and tapped my foot. No one addressed us. Larry kept looking at his watch and shaking his head. A few minutes after

4:00, I approached the reception desk and asked how much longer we should expect to wait.

"Not much longer, probably," said the woman behind the desk, without looking up. *Probably? Well, that was helpful,* I thought. I sat back down.

"What did she say?" asked Larry.

"She told me we'd better plan on sleeping here tonight," I replied.

"What?"

"Mrs. Kaplan?" a voice called. Finally! Of course, they hadn't read the forms where I'd filled in my title as "Dr.," not "Mrs." Mrs. Kaplan is Larry's mother. But I answered anyway.

"Yes!"

"Follow me," said a young woman in surgical scrubs. Larry and I got up and followed her through a wooden door into a tiled corridor. She led us into an exam room, a brightly lit cubicle much like the one in Dr. Goodman's office. She weighed me, took my blood pressure, pulse, and temperature, and gave me a gown to put on. She left the room saying, "Dr. Payne should be with you shortly."

After another 15 or 20 minutes, Dr. Payne, a rumpled, slightly overweight man of about 40, entered and introduced himself. He made no eye contact and did not acknowledge our long wait. He peered at my chart.

"Well, it appears that you do have hepatitis C," he confirmed. "You will need some further blood tests to confirm the diagnosis and rule out other diseases of the liver, which are unlikely, if you want to get treated. Then you'll need a liver biopsy before you can begin treatment."

"Can you explain the treatment to us?" I asked.

Dr. Payne went through a long explanation of alpha interferon, the drug he was testing in his experimental protocol. Apparently, everyone in the study got the drug for six months. It was injected below the skin three times a week, in the leg, arm, or belly. It had some significant side effects of fatigue, fever, and flu-like symptoms, and worked by boosting the immune system to put the virus in check. So far, about 50 percent of the patients taking the drug responded to it with improvement in their liver function tests, but only half of those patients—so, 25 percent in all—had long-term improvement. Dr. Payne and his team were hoping to collect more data on response rates and side effects.

"So I have only a twenty-five percent chance of really getting better on this medicine?" I asked.

"Yes, it looks that way. But it's all we have right now," he replied, rather dispassionately.

"Well, what happens if I don't get better? I have a seven-month-old son."

"The biopsy will tell us how much liver damage you have. But prognosis is a difficult thing. You could have minimal damage now, but the disease could suddenly accelerate later. Or you might live with it for years without much trouble. In most people with mild disease, it takes up to twenty years to get cirrhosis. So you'll probably be alive to see your son graduate high school."

Was he serious? Was that supposed to make me feel better? I did a quick calculation in my head. I'd be 48 when Max graduated from high school. I needed to be around a lot longer than that! Did he really think that was as long as I'd live?

Dr. Payne addressed Larry. "Do you have any questions right now?"

Larry asked about the liver biopsy—when and where it would be done. Dr. Payne informed us that I would have to stay overnight in a part of the hospital called the Clinical Research Unit for observation, but that I shouldn't worry about that yet, since the blood test results would take several weeks to come back, and they needed to be reviewed before we arranged the biopsy.

Finally, I asked about sex. Since hepatitis C was a communicable disease, I was taking precautions not to expose anyone to my blood. I was covering cuts immediately and being vigilant about capping my razor at home and putting my toothbrush away so Larry didn't use it accidentally. I'd read different things about sexual exposure. The Centers for Disease Control had not yet made a firm statement about protection as it had for hepatitis B and HIV; for both those diseases, safer sex practices were recommended regardless of monogamy. Although I asked the question, Dr. Payne clearly directed his answer to Larry.

He recounted an experiment that was done with hepatitis C–infected female chimpanzees and uninfected male chimpanzees. I don't recall his exact words, but they were something like "the uninfected males screwed like crazy with the infected females and none of them became infected." This again was meant to be reassuring. And no, I wasn't exactly offended by his language, but there was something in the way he told the story. Maybe the word I'm looking for is *conspiratorially,* as though he and Larry were two guys out for a beer, talking about how to score. I felt uncomfortable. But I reminded myself to try to take the information as it was intended and leave it at that. Dr. Payne's bedside manner left something to be desired, but I needed his knowledge, not his empathy.

We wrapped up the appointment with instructions for all the blood tests. He directed us to the lab and told us the office would be in touch when the results were available. *So this is how it feels,* I thought. *Now I'm not in control. Or shall I say, now I know I'm not in control.*

CHAPTER 4

# What We Keep and What Gets Left Behind

I'D LOVE TO be able to say that Dr. Payne was completely awful. That he was just a mean man with terrible bedside manner. But it wasn't that simple. I think he was a very smart, rather shy man who was doing his best to help me, that he was limited in his capacity for empathy, and that I was a particularly difficult patient for him.

I think I challenged Dr. Payne in ways that made him feel inadequate and unable to help me. As a very cerebral kind of doctor, a guy who was a lot more comfortable in the lab than in the consultation room, he may not have thought through what to do when he didn't know the answers to the questions his patients posed. Instead of admitting the limitations of the current body of knowledge and then offering what he could, Dr. Payne became distant and defensive. I'm sure the fact of my being a physician and asking more complicated questions than the average patient played a role. But medical knowledge notwithstanding, it had to have been tremendously difficult to answer questions that patients posed about hepatitis C in those early days after the virus was isolated. If the questions could be answered at all, the answers were not terribly encouraging.

I wanted to know how I got the virus and how long I'd had it. There was no way to answer. I wanted to know my prognosis. Again, no answer. And I wanted to know whether medication would work for me. Only a 25 percent chance. Not very encouraging. I think that something Dr. Payne truly didn't understand was the idea that doctors can offer patients comfort and optimism without offering false hope. It is not always in words, but in the way the body is angled, in the eyes, in the touch of a shoulder that this salve is offered. And patients who are physicians are not immune to its effects. Perhaps we who have seen the worst need that soothing most of all.

I'd also love to slam the whole medical training system and say that it encourages the development of unkind, hardened, jaded doctors. While I believe that there is a little piece of truth in those assertions, I don't think it's really The Truth. If it were that simple, every doctor coming out of residency training would be inhumane, and clearly that is not the case. Reality is so much more complicated because it involves human beings, and human beings are tremendously variable.

Medical training does take young, idealistic students and expose them to years of rote memorization, sleep deprivation, slave-wage labor, high-pressure situations, and sometimes humiliation. However, these circumstances are more the by-products of the training than the education itself.

When I started medical school, I was full of idealism and optimism and plans to be cutting-edge in my knowledge but also a real healer. The University of Pennsylvania School of Medicine did a pretty good job of maintaining that idealism on the whole; the students, at least when I was there, were protected from abuse. Our education took precedence over the "slave labor" tasks that the interns and residents often use students for in other institutions. We weren't humiliated in the anatomy lab or on rounds. But the workload was massive, and it was challenging. I did realize that I would never know it all, and I wondered whether I would ever know enough. Still, my mission was intact when I reached my internship.

For internship and residency, I chose to enter "the trenches" at Temple University Hospital. Temple is Philadelphia's version of Bellevue in Manhattan. It serves an indigent population within an area of the city that is embattled with drug abuse and gang violence. The emergency room is full of gunshot wounds and heroin overdoses on a typical evening. There are many faculty members in the hospital who are sought out by patients outside the neighborhood, and the hospital also serves the very large university population, so there is a mixed bag of patients, but back in the 1980s, when I was a resident, Temple had a distinctly different feel from the Hospital of the University of Pennsylvania (HUP). I felt I would get a more practical education there, with perhaps less esoteric, specialized training and more hard-core, "real" medicine.

The real draw for me at Temple was that the residents "ran the show" with oversight from the attendings, who, it was said, intervened only when absolutely necessary. Fellows, the doctors in subspecialty training one step above residency, generally had little to do with us; they were there to learn invasive procedures and do research, unlike at HUP, where they were often in charge.

This autonomy of the interns and residents turned out to be a double-edged sword. It was something we all thought we wanted going in, but reality wasn't always what I'd imagined. From the beginning, it was clear that we would all bond tightly to each other, and we had a camaraderie that must have been a bit like what soldiers feel: we were interdependent, clinging to each other for dear life at times—and not always our own lives. As interns, we had to call on our upper-year residents to save lives all the time, because we simply didn't know what we were doing, and they had to tell us or show us what to do.

We used the "see one, do one, teach one" method, so after a month or so, we interns were calling on each other, as well. If one person knew how to do something particularly well, word would get around. The first interns to rotate through the intensive care units had experience with central line (large IV lines directly into the major blood vessels) placement and emergency resuscitation. I was the best at spinal taps, having had a meningitis patient in my first block. If we could avoid calling our senior resident, and at all costs avoid calling the attending, that was best; there was a tacit rule that asking for help showed weakness. Yet we were certainly expected to know when we needed help; overstepping our limits was clearly frowned upon, so it was a fine line.

I don't believe it was our faculty attendings who promoted the concept that asking for help indicated weakness. To the contrary, I think they were standing by, and most would have welcomed calls. At least I say this in retrospect, and it comes from an insider's view, as I now know many of those very same professors as colleagues and social contacts. At the time, I had no way of knowing this, because my education was coming primarily from other residents. The lore came from them. In all honesty, though, when I did have to call an attending, I almost always got a friendly greeting, a receptive ear, and helpful advice.

The problem with retrospect is that what one remembers most vividly is the dramatic or the traumatic. Most of hospital care was quite routine. Underneath the routine, of course, were the daily dramas of my patients' lives, but the care itself was methodical, detail-oriented, and often slow and grueling, rather than the fast-paced calamities shown on television. Most often, patients improved and were discharged. Occasionally they didn't improve or they died. The few events that shaped us for better or worse lay etched deep in our memory.

I can recall one very positive interaction with a favorite faculty attending, Dr. Wise, a wonderful teacher, who always had positive feedback for us on rounds and knew how to add some clinical wisdom without making us feel that he was taking our power away. During Christmas week of my internship year, my team was on holiday call, with half the usual house staff in the hospital so that people could be home with their families. I was on call for the day, and Dr. Wise was making rounds with me and my third-year resident, who was about to go home for the afternoon. Things were quiet with our patients, except for one particularly troubling case, a young woman with mysterious symptoms, including loss of blood flow to her fingertips. She was developing something that looked like frostbite and was slowly progressing to gangrene, though she had not been exposed to the cold, and she was at risk of losing her fingertips. Many tests had been done, and we were still waiting for some results, but no diagnosis had been made yet. Time was running out.

I'd stayed up late the night before, researching my patient's plight. I'd copied an article about an experimental treatment used in a similar situation: direct injection of a substance that dilates blood vessels into the radial artery in the wrist. I showed it to Dr. Wise.

"What do you think?" I asked him.

"I think your patient is running out of options. If you'd like to try this, and the pharmacy can supply you with the medication, I'll take responsibility," he told me.

I was tremendously excited. If it worked, my patient's fingers would be saved, and she'd be only the second person ever to receive such a treatment. I could write up the case! But if it didn't...The potential problems were myriad. She could become hypotensive if too much of the medication got in her bloodstream. Her artery could be damaged. Still, I had to try. I got the pharmacy to mix up the meds. I explained the procedure to the patient and got her consent.

When the time came to start the patient's arterial infusion, however, I froze. Here I was, an intern, only months out of medical school, doing experiments on a real, live human being. I was all alone with her, in a hospital on half-staff because of the holiday. I went out to the nurse's station and called Dr. Wise at home.

"Roz, I think we should do it," he said.

"Easy for you to say. You're not here watching if something goes wrong. I'm scared!"

"Okay. Go back in her room, and call me from the phone in there. I'll stay on the phone with you while you do the procedure. If anything goes wrong, I'll come right back to the hospital."

So he sat in his living room listening as I infused the vasodilator into my patient's wrist. In the end, it didn't save her fingers, but it also did no harm.

A couple of days later, a blood test yielded a diagnosis. She had some rare antibodies in her blood that were causing an autoimmune reaction. A procedure called plasmapheresis ultimately helped her.

Not all my interactions with my superiors were as positive as the one with Dr. Wise. There were some attendings who were not good role models and who left me wondering what had happened to them in their own career paths.

I'll call my oncology attending Dr. Addams, for her resemblance to Morticia Addams. She was tall and thin and unnaturally pale, with long, jet-black hair. She favored bohemian skirts and T-shirts, and a pair of purple, fringed boots that channeled the early 1970s. I didn't feel as though I was learning very much from her in my rotation on the oncology unit. She preferred talking about her research or obscure tumors to either the cases at hand or the treatment of the "usual" cancers that we needed to master. But my most serious criticism of Dr. Addams was that, despite the fact that she was a cancer doctor, she rarely talked about pain or death or end-of-life issues.

I wanted to ease through that month of oncology in the spring of my internship year and avoid any personal interaction with Dr. Addams. But the night Mr. Clark started bleeding would make that impossible.

A dark stain seeped into the sheet where he'd lain. I had been able to roll Mr. Clark toward me in his hospital bed without help; he was so wasted and frail, it felt as though I were moving a small child. Another stain covering the lower back of his hospital gown coalesced into a crimson pool with the mark on the bed. The unmistakable, metallic stench of melena, the bloody stool of a lower gastrointestinal bleed, filled the room. Mr. Clark moaned incoherently.

*Damn!* I thought to myself. *There's the explanation for his low blood pressure.* It was 11:30 on a Wednesday night. I was covering the oncology unit and two other medical floors. Just two days earlier, Mr. Clark, an 82-year-old gentleman, had been transferred to our oncology unit from another floor, after he'd been diagnosed with lymphoma. Tonight, the nurse in the oncology unit had called me to examine Mr. Clark because she'd found him semiconscious, with very low blood pressure. Of course, the nurse hadn't realized he was bleeding from his rectum. It had probably been going on for several hours, and he'd already lost a large amount of blood.

I began resuscitation. Of course, I first called for help, but it was a busy night on call, and we were stretched pretty thin. My fellow interns and my supervising resident were involved in their own patient crises and were unavailable. The only way to get other doctors there immediately would be to call a "code blue," interrupting all other hospital care and procedures. This was not quite a code blue situation, at least not yet. My resident said he'd come as soon as he could, but it might be a while. I yelled out into the hall for a nurse, and for IV equipment. Two large-bore IV lines. Type and cross. Run fluids in as fast as they'll go. Call for a bed in intensive care. Send lab tests. Start the blood running in. Call the radiology fellow to beg for a bleeding scan so we can find out where the blood is coming from.

Only after all this was done did I call Dr. Addams. The reason I called was that I wanted her to consider a "do not resuscitate" order for Mr. Clark. DNR orders had to come from the attending, not the resident. I had already tried to contact Mr. Clark's family without success. There was only a nephew listed as a contact, and he was not answering his phone. It would be up to the attending to make a decision, since Mr. Clark could not speak for himself.

In fact, when Mr. Clark came to our unit, my resident and I expressed concern that he was too frail to start chemotherapy, and that he was likely to experience complications. I was upset that Dr. Addams chose a very aggressive drug regimen, but when I asked her why, she brushed me off. She didn't address our worries about complications. We wanted to review the complications with Mr. Clark and ask him about his "code status"—that is, his wishes regarding mechanical ventilation and resuscitation if something were to go wrong. But Dr. Addams told us to wait. She said to "give it some time," so that Mr. Clark would not reject the idea of chemo. And because she was the attending, we had to listen.

So here I was, putting in a call to Dr. Addams at home, hoping for a DNR order now that the horse was already out of the barn. The phone rang a few times on her end, and a man's voice, edged with annoyance, answered. I introduced myself and asked for Dr. Addams.

"Well, she's not here, and I can't tell you when she'll be in. I suggest you page her," he told me. I thanked the voice and hung up.

Dr. Addams didn't answer her pages, either. As an intern, it was hard for me to fathom. I hadn't turned off my pager since July first, even on my nights off, and I couldn't imagine failing to respond to a page. As I continued to tend to Mr. Clark's vital signs and transfuse him, holding the bags of blood high in the air and squeezing them to make the blood run in faster, I repeatedly paged Dr. Addams and waited, hoping she would respond. Finally, with the last unit of blood running in, I called her house again. It was almost 2 A.M. Again, the annoyed man said she wasn't home.

"It's a serious emergency. I really need to reach her immediately. Is there anywhere else I might find her?" I asked.

"I wish I knew," he said, now sounding more defeated than annoyed. "But I'll give her the message when she gets home."

My beeper went off, startling me out of a moment I was taking to contemplate other ways to get the DNR order. I called back the number displayed: the radiology suite. They were ready to start Mr. Clark's bleeding scan. I reviewed his vital signs and his latest stat labs. He was stable enough to move downstairs to radiology, but just barely. The blood and IV fluids continued to run wide open, and all the medications that could be given to decrease bleeding had already been administered. My resident was still tied up in the emergency room, so I was still on my own. I recruited an ICU nurse to help me transport the patient. This was as good as it was going to get.

Before we began the trip downstairs, I stood close to Mr. Clark and looked down at him. His eyes were open. I told him what had happened to him and what we were about to do.

"Do you understand?" I asked.

He seemed to look at me. He may have nodded; I wasn't sure. He didn't speak. His eyes were hollow. I knew already that he was going to die. I wondered whether he knew it, or if he was already gone, really. I knew he was alone, but I just hoped he wasn't in pain, or frightened. He didn't look frightened, but how could I tell? I didn't know this man.

The nurse pushed the gurney down the hall while I pushed the IV pole and continued to squeeze the bag with the blood. We'd had to disconnect Mr. Clark's heart monitor—we didn't have portable heart monitors back then—but I frequently reached down to feel his pulse. It remained steady.

The radiology fellow was waiting for us. The nurse helped us move our patient onto the steel table in the nuclear medicine room and then fled back to intensive care. For a while, I kept monitoring Mr. Clark, while the fellow injected the radioactive scan material and got the equipment set up. Then he sent me out of the room to watch from behind a glass window while he performed the study.

A bleeding scan tracks the flow of blood through the arteries; the idea is that when the radioactive tracer left the circulatory system and entered the gastrointestinal tract, we would know the exact site of bleeding. Then a course of action could be taken medically or surgically to correct it. But the test is long and burdensome, and Mr. Clark did not stay completely still. He was apparently uncomfortable on the steel table, and even slight movement could cause artifacts in the scan. The radiologist was a bit frustrated. An hour went by. I became anxious about my patient's status; I had no way to know whether his blood pressure and pulse were stable. I continued to try to call my resident for help. He was still busy. I tried to call Mr. Clark's nephew again. Still no answer. I watched through the glass. I looked at my watch. Somehow it was nearly 5 A.M.

I opened the door to the room and asked the fellow if I could check Mr. Clark's vital signs.

"I'm nearly done," he said. "Just wait another five minutes. He's started to settle down and I'm getting good films now."

But it wasn't good that Mr. Clark had started to settle down. He was *too* still.

"Stop," I said. "If he dies, good films aren't going to help us."

I grabbed Mr. Clark's arm. His pulse was barely palpable. I picked up a blood pressure cuff. No pressure. His breathing was shallow.

"Call a code."

By the time the other medical interns and residents arrived, there was no pulse and I had started CPR. We followed procedure. Three rounds of epinephrine. Atropine. Intubation. None of it mattered. Mr. Clark bled out on a steel table in the radiology suite with a bunch of doctors-in-training pounding on his chest. I doubt it's what he would have wanted, but nobody ever asked him what he wanted, as far as I could tell.

When it was all over, and the crowd dispersed, an unnatural quiet filled the room. Only my upper-year resident and I remained in the radiology suite with the body. We removed the tubes and IV lines and covered Mr. Clark with a sheet. Finally transport came to move him to the morgue. My resident went off to finish an admission in the emergency room. I stood alone, immobilized, feeling ice-cold. I was unsure whether it was actually cold in the room or if something inside of me was causing me to shiver.

My beeper interrupted my inertia. It was 7 A.M. and other interns had arrived. My friend Jerry was paging me to get sign-out from the night. I told him to meet me in the residents' lounge.

"What happened to you?" he asked loudly, looking me up and down and frowning. Jerry always looked like he'd slept in his clothes, so it was disconcerting to have him look at me that way. I was usually well groomed, and even after a night on call I ordinarily showered and dressed, unlike many of the interns, who stayed in their surgical scrubs until attending rounds in the late morning, when they were required to appear in "appropriate" attire. This morning, I was not only still in my surgical scrubs and a rumpled white coat, but those garments were splattered with blood and smeared with feces from my hands-on care of Mr. Clark. Besides that, my hair had been hastily tied back in a messy ponytail, which was coming undone, and my skin was sallow from lack of sleep.

Until Jerry's remark, I hadn't realized how bad I looked, and probably smelled.

"I can't explain. I just came from a code. I mean he died. My patient. He bled out." I was crying now, full force, something I'd never done before in front of one of my colleagues. Jerry looked alarmed.

"Who was the patient?" he asked.

"One of the onc. unit patients. He had lymphoma, and he

was on one of Dr. Addams's protocols. He should have had a DNR. I couldn't get the DNR."

"You know it's not your fault. It sounds like he was just going to die. He was a cancer patient. They die. Patients die. You need to go get some coffee and change your clothes before work rounds."

"Yeah," I said, wiping my face and sniffing. I gave him his sign-out. I knew it wasn't my fault. I also knew Jerry wouldn't understand. It's not that the patient died. It's not *if* you die, it's *how* you die, I wanted to say. But I knew it wouldn't make a difference.

As it turned out, I had no time for coffee or clean clothes. I had to put out a few small fires before work rounds. And it was Thursday, the day Dr. Addams showed up for early-morning work rounds. *Ugh.*

I got there just in time. Dr. Addams stood on 7 East with my resident, Sharon; the other oncology unit intern, Dan; and the medical students, next to a metal cart containing our patient charts. I felt five pairs of eyes staring at my stained scrubs and coat, my red eyes and puffy face. I had to launch directly into an explanation of the events of the previous night, since we had lost a patient from our service.

"Yes," said Dr. Addams, "I heard this morning that you called me at home about Mr. Clark, it's very unfortunate. Do you think there's anything you could have done differently?"

"Well, I think it would have been better for the patient if he had had a DNR order," I said.

"But he didn't," Dr. Addams stated.

"No."

"So you did what needed to be done, and the outcome was poor. Unfortunately, GI bleeding can be a complication of chemotherapy. Did the patient get the appropriate care?"

I knew the answer she was looking for, and I was going to have to give it to her. But I was sleep-deprived, and hungry, and in caffeine withdrawal. The "yes" came out with a new onslaught of tears. I managed to contain it within a few seconds, but it was already too late.

"I want to see you in my office later. Make sure you've showered and changed by then. Two P.M., third floor of the Medical Office Building. Room 308."

I pushed through rounds and all my post-call patient care on a caffeine buzz and automatic pilot. Fortunately, the work was routine and there were no unforeseen events. I arrived in the Medical Office Building, a dingy structure tacked on to a far corner of the hospital, right on time. Dr. Addams's office door was open, and she sat behind her oversized, messy desk in a cinder-block cubicle with a green tile floor. Under the harsh fluorescent light, her face appeared especially pallid, her dry, frizzy dark hair in stark contrast to it. She motioned me in and told me to sit.

"Thanks for coming in," she began. "I was concerned by your behavior this morning. I'm concerned that you're not dealing with death well."

At first I wondered whether I'd heard her wrong. Then a thousand responses flashed through my mind. Where had she been the night before? Why hadn't she called me back? If she had answered my calls, perhaps Mr. Clark would have been spared unnecessary suffering. And what was wrong with crying in the face of such an awful, violent, lonely death?

But I was suddenly exhausted, way too exhausted to speak. No words would come out. And really, what was the point in saying any of this to Dr. Addams? She would think whatever she wanted to anyway. Instead, I would tell her something she could understand.

"Dr. Addams, it's not death that I'm having a problem with," I said. "It's life. My life. I was tired and hungry and covered in blood and stool. I'm sorry for disrupting rounds."

"Oh. Well. If that's all, then go finish your work. I just…"

"Well, thanks," I said, and got up to go.

Leaving her office, I felt curiously free, as if I'd dodged a bullet. I hadn't let her tell me not to care. My soul was intact. As I headed back to 7 East for sign-out rounds, I wondered whether the nurses had reached Mr. Clark's nephew yet. I wondered who would come to his funeral and what they would say about the man who was Mr. Clark before he became a patient.

While I may have wanted to avoid the counsel of Dr. Addams to "distance myself," in retrospect, I may have benefited from some version of her advice. I was never in danger of losing my empathy. Toning it down just a little probably would have been in my own best interest, since, if anything, I always felt too much. An experience I had as a second-year resident epitomized this.

In the second year, we spent one month at a small outlying hospital, and a single resident was left at night to cover the medical patients. One night when I was in charge there, a patient developed a dangerously rapid heart rate. The usual drugs did not resolve it, and his blood pressure dropped. He was semiconscious and moaning. I had to shock him with the defibrillator. The first shock was a failure. So was the second. I had the nurse stat-page the cardiologist, and he barked instructions over the phone to me: "Give him some Brevitol and shock him again." I did what he said. The patient jerked violently with the shock. No change.

"Turn the voltage up on the defibrillator," the cardiologist instructed. I followed his instructions until the patient's heart finally returned to a normal rhythm and his blood pressure stabilized. It took nine shocks in all. Afterward, I was short of breath and my chest ached, as though I myself had received the shocks.

Throughout the entire encounter, what I wanted most was to run away. I was in a panic, and the adrenaline surge was so overwhelming that I felt not motivated, but terrorized. Perhaps this kind of over-empathizing could have led me to block out feelings, to shut down, but it didn't. It served as another reminder of how much I still needed to learn, and how much I disliked being alone in an emergency, but I kept on feeling.

I don't want to paint a false picture of myself, however, as being constantly sensitive to the feelings of others. Like every trainee, I did some things I'm not proud of. As interns, we were under pressure and "low man on the totem pole" among the doctors, so we'd take that out on whomever we could. My rule: it just couldn't be the patients.

One night, another intern, Katie, and I were covering two adjacent medical floors and sharing an on-call room. At about 3 A.M. we'd finally flopped on the beds in the on-call room after a hellish evening of "scut (Some Common Unfinished Task) work" and "code blues." Just as we were drifting off, Katie's beeper paged her. One of the nurses, a young woman from India who wore the traditional sari at work, asked for pain medication for a patient on the medical floor. Katie looked through her patient list.

"That patient isn't on my list. One of the other interns must be responsible for him."

"Oh, Doctor, he is your patient. His chart has a red dot," she replied, referring to a color-coding system we had devised to avoid just such confusion.

"Well," said Katie, "You have a red dot and *you're* not my patient!" and she hung up the phone.

We both laughed hysterically, doubled over, and fell off our beds. It was laughter without mirth. Xenophobia had become riotously funny to us in our stuporous exhaustion. My colleague was lucky the nurse didn't report her. The nurse had probably found the comment too humiliating to discuss. I still wince at the cruelty we were reduced to. Even worse, I doubt the patient ever got his pain medication. But I didn't carry this kind of behavior away as a core part of my being.

What I remember most from training is feeling scared. I felt that I might not know what to do or how to do it and that as a result, a patient would suffer. Nights always felt perilous, stretching on with infinite possibilities for disaster. I remember the relief I felt passing the big plate-glass windows across from the elevators and seeing the sun come up in the early mornings, because it meant that help was on the way.

Did the fear serve a purpose? It kept me on my toes, yes, but I think I should have had better supervision, and I guess I have some anger about that. We worked in a macho system that rewarded toughness. We didn't admit that we felt inadequate, and we didn't admit what we didn't know. I know the system has improved and that supervision has tightened up. I hope the current trainees don't feel as frightened as I did. Still, I walked out of the program with confidence, self-sufficiency, and a good bit of knowledge. I also am quite certain that my empathy was intact and that I still knew how to be kind and respectful to patients.

I imagine that Dr. Payne's medical training wasn't that different from my own. He trained in an urban university medical center. He wasn't that much older than I. He probably had many similar experiences to mine, and I'm sure, like me, he encountered a variety of helpful and harmful role models. But I have no idea how he processed these experiences and how they shaped him. Was he also frightened and unsure, or was he brash and unflappable? Did he identify with his patients, or did he shut down his personal feelings and reactions? Did he have guidance from his superiors and support from his peers, or was he damaged by isolation during his early clinical years? I'll never know how Dr. Payne came to be the kind of doctor he was, or how the chasm between us formed, given the amount of common ground we should have shared.

It's hard for me to find the right doctor these days. It's not just because of Dr. Payne, or other past relationships I've had with doctors, some of which have been very healing. But the relationship between doctor and patient is so fragile, my own care of my patients sometimes so deficient, so much less than what I'd meant for it to be. How does anyone trust?

# CHAPTER 5

# Before the Fall

I HAVE TO THINK hard to remember married life, or my relationship with Larry at all, for that matter, before hepatitis C. Come to think of it, there were a host of misfortunes that struck in those early years of our marriage, coloring them with such intensity that the bride and groom in our wedding album seem to be people we were hardly acquainted with. But when I do make the effort to think back, I think I remember being happy. Yes, I'm pretty sure we were.

We met in Larry's living room. No great mystery to this. He was a fourth-year med student at Temple and shared an apartment in a big old stone house in Mount Airy with two other med students and a medical intern. I was a third-year med student at the University of Pennsylvania, and my friend Beth met Larry's intern housemate, Zach, on one of her rotations at an outside hospital. They were dating, and one snowy winter evening, I tagged along to Zach's house with Beth to watch a movie. Zach was the only person we knew with a VCR back then.

Halfway through *Entre Nous,* a 1980s drama about an intense friendship between two women, Larry came stomping in, carrying cross-country skis and shaking off snow. He apparently had been completing a shift at the local food co-op and had used his skis for transportation. Zach made introductions.

*Cute,* I thought, surveying his dark curls and mischievous blue eyes behind glasses with bright red frames (that was Larry's trademark in the '80s). *But way too granola for me. Food co-ops? Cross-country skis for transportation? Bet he wears Birkenstocks with his scrubs!* (He did).

Larry sat down next to me on the sofa to watch the rest of the movie.

The living room of the old house was drafty and cold. Larry would later tell me that they kept the house at 60 degrees because they couldn't afford the heating bill. I'd been freezing, despite two pairs of socks and two sweaters, the whole evening. After sitting with Larry for a while and chatting in between scenes of the movie, I somehow ended up with my feet tucked under him for warmth. It wasn't premeditated and we didn't talk about it. I just felt so comfortable with him that it happened almost unconsciously. Of course, Larry took this as a sign that I was open to seeing him again, and at the end of the evening he asked me to dinner for the next week.

We'd been dating for several months when a conversation about our childhoods led to the realization that our parents had lived in the same town and belonged to the same synagogue when we were babies. They had some common friends. Doubtless, we had shared a playpen at some gathering or other between the ages of zero and three, before my family moved away. I've always wondered whether our instant bond and sense of familiarity was borne out of some deeply rooted preverbal memory, rather than just serendipity.

Already in the clinical years of medical school, Larry and I both had long hours at the hospital and sometimes all-night shifts by the time we met. We had patient care responsibilities and academic commitments that we took very seriously. Life was already different for us than it was for most young couples, but we were still relatively carefree, compared to the years to come. Larry had already applied to internal medicine residency programs before we became a couple. Residencies and applicants are "matched" nationwide by computer according to the preferences of both the programs and the applicants. Larry's first choice was the University of Michigan Hospital. Luckily for us, the program didn't place him high enough on their list for him to match there. He landed in his second-choice residency, the Medical College of Pennsylvania, which kept him in Philly and gave our relationship a chance to grow. The following year, when I applied to internal medicine residencies, I applied only to Philadelphia programs, since by then we knew we wanted to stay together.

I imagine that a relationship in which only one partner is in medicine is very difficult for the nonmedical partner. He or she would need a lot of patience and forbearance and, one would hope, many other people to be with. The wife of a cantankerous elderly doctor I know was holding court with a bunch of her husband's residents and fellows at a hospital fundraiser recently. I heard her say, "I bet you all wonder how I've lived with The Doctor all these years." There were some snickers and nods. She went on.

"I just really like my own company!"

She got quite a laugh, but it rang true, especially with a man of that generation, who not only put in the work hours but also spent his social time with his peers. Any doctor, especially during the intense period of training, sinks into the world of medicine completely. There is time and energy for little else. The advantage Larry and I, and other medical couples, have is that we have always understood the priorities and the commitments. Of course, our loved ones come first now, and they did then as well, but short of emergent need from those loved ones, we were committed to those hours in the hospital, and during training there were a lot of them.

And it wasn't just the hours. It was the way we were absorbed. The way it consumed us, the way in which we were completely used up by our work much of the time. And the way in which we were passionate toward our work. We loved it, we struggled with it, sometimes we abhorred it; we rejoiced in it, we dreaded it, we cried over it, we reveled in it. It expanded our minds, it tore us to shreds, it made us proud, and it brought us to our knees. But never, never, never were we bored by it.

Larry and I always had different ways of coping with the stresses of medicine. This showed up very early in our careers. During internship and residency, I took every situation very seriously and worried over details. Larry took a lighter view and used humor to get through difficult moments. I remember coming home from a night early in my internship and recounting the events to Larry.

"Right after my team signed out, my beeper went off and one of the nurses on Seven East tells me 'Patient 746 by the door—dead!' She didn't even know his name!" I had used my best Indian accent, which probably sounded more like I was from New Jersey than Bombay.

"So I asked, 'Is he supposed to be dead?' It turned out he was expected to die, but I can't believe I said that, it's so sick and inhumane! And then I got called down to the ER and walked past the trauma room and there's this gunshot wound and the trauma surgeons are working behind the curtain. There's blood all over the floor and people yelling and all, and outside the curtain is a cop and he's got the suspect handcuffed to him. Only the guy is wearing a short leather jacket and nothing else, standing there in the middle of the ER.

"So then I go by the nurses' station to get to ER Room Six and next to the nurses' station is this old man on a stretcher, drinking his own urine out of a urinal…"

Larry burst out laughing. But I wanted to cry.

"Don't you see the humor in it?" he asked me.

"No, it's all awful," I wailed. "It's dehumanizing and pathetic!"

It wasn't that Larry wasn't as sensitive as I was to the sadness of it all. He just knew something I didn't—that sinking into it didn't help anyone. Later, I would stop noticing all the extreme suffering and bizarre behavior as I went about my business in the hospital. I had to become inured to it to remain effective in my work.

Larry's lighter approach helped him get by, though it did get him in some trouble occasionally. Once, he admitted a patient who had choked on a piece of meat and had to have it removed endoscopically. Along with his other orders for the patient, he wrote one for 'Adolph's meat tenderizer to bedside.'

This amused the nurses to no end but got Larry a slap on the wrist from a supervisor. On another occasion, when a passive-aggressive nurse insisted on paging him repeatedly during the night for a patient's diarrhea that he had already treated, he ordered standing and squatting stool velocities. It took the nurse some time to figure out that "stool velocities" would require a stopwatch and a mathematical formula; and they had a talk and a good laugh together later.

Larry's best friend, Lee, dyed his hair red, white, and blue for their rotation through the V.A. hospital. The two of them, along with another resident, became dismayed after a week at the facility when they realized how many of the patients were there simply waiting for nursing home placement. They built a "veteran" out of balloons, a V.A. bathrobe, and a Foley catheter filled with coffee, placed it in a wheelchair, and pinned to its chest a sign saying "Please Place Me". During a night shift, they wheeled it into the administration office and left it there. Of course, the political prank was traced back to them and they were duly chastised. Still, they benefited from the ability to get the issue off their chests in a lighthearted way.

Meanwhile, I suffered each injustice and every social plight I witnessed with horror. I often bottled up the feelings and I was much too afraid of authority to pull any pranks.

Not only did I take the emotional part of doctoring hard, but it soon became obvious that I was not well suited to the physical challenges, either. Some people, Larry included, managed well on very little sleep and didn't suffer the effects of a missed meal very much. But for me, every missed meal meant a headache and dizziness. Less than four hours' sleep in a night and I would spend the next day with a pain in my solar plexus, burning eyes, back and neck pain, nausea, and a variety of other ailments. If it weren't for Larry, I might not have made it through my internship year. After a night on call and working until 6:00 or so the next evening, I would come home and immediately fall into a heavy, dreamless sleep. He would wake me at about 9 P.M. and force-feed me a grilled cheese sandwich and tomato soup, the only meal he knew how to make. Then he'd turn on a movie and try to keep me awake for an hour or two to normalize my sleep pattern. The next time I was to be on call, I'd tell him I couldn't do another night, and he'd tell me I could, that I'd make it through. He'd send me back to the hospital, a trainer sending his boxer back into the ring for another round.

Needless to say, we didn't have much time to see each other during our internship and residency years, since during our internships we were on call every third night, and during the two years of residency following, we were on every fourth night. We were in different hospitals and rarely on the same call schedule. Yet somehow we made time. Sometimes one of us would drop by the other's hospital at dinnertime (we'd page each other first, to check that no emergency was in progress). If we had a weekend day off together, we'd devote the whole day to each other. It was never enough, but it had to do. We ended up getting engaged during a five-minute break in the action at the hospital.

We had been living in separate apartments in Mount Airy but spending most of our nights together, and neither apartment was large enough for two. The search for a new apartment had been slow because of our time constraints, but one

Saturday we located one that we agreed was close to perfect. Larry was going to sign the lease on Sunday while I was on call in the ICU.

Late that Sunday morning, I was busy trying to stabilize a man bleeding profusely from a gastric ulcer when my beeper paged me to an outside call. The nurse took over for a minute while I answered the phone. It was Larry, saying he was having second thoughts about the apartment. It was too far from the medical college hospital, where he worked, he said. I had no time to talk, I told him, but we really couldn't spend more time looking at apartments, and maybe he just couldn't make the commitment to moving in together. The icy tone I gave him was unmistakable; he knew he was in the doghouse. I hung up and went back to my patient.

The bleeding came under control and I set about the thousand other tasks I had caring for the other patients in the ICU. Around noon, Larry appeared, a pint of Ben and Jerry's Super Fudge Chunk ice cream in his hand.

"We need to talk," he said.

"Well, as you can see, I'm a little busy right now."

"Five minutes," he pleaded.

"I can't leave the unit," I told him. "I've got a bleeder I have to watch, and unstable patients on ventilators. And there's no privacy here." There were nurses and other doctors milling about at the nurses' station.

"Well, there must be someplace..." he said.

I looked around, then took his hand and dragged him toward a door. As I opened it, a strong smell of antiseptic blasted out at us. It was the supply closet. I peeked around as we snuck in and closed the door. Nobody seemed to notice us. I flipped on the light switch.

"What is it?" I hissed at him angrily.

"Well, you know how you said I wasn't committed?"

"Yeah?"

"Well, you're wrong. Ask me to marry you."

"What?" I asked. I thought he was playing one of his pranks. The "M" word had not been discussed in our relationship. I'd always figured it would come up eventually, but living together had seemed enough of a commitment at the time.

"Ask me to marry you," he repeated.

"Come on, stop fooling around. I told you I don't have time for this now!"

"So just ask me, and then I'll give you the ice cream and leave you alone."

"Fine, will you marry me," I said flatly, impatiently.

"Yes."

"Good, now leave."

He handed me the pint of ice cream (my favorite flavor) and we left the closet. He strode out of the ICU. I put the ice cream in the freezer in the little kitchenette and went back to work, but I was a bit distracted. Part of me thought Larry had been joking. And that's the way I'd tell it in future years to our friends, that I thought it was a joke. But a deeper part of me knew that he would never make fun of something as important as our feelings for each other. In my heart, I realized that in Larry's eccentric little way, he had just proposed to me.

I called him later that evening and asked him if he'd been serious. I got a deadpan "Of course I was." I couldn't be

100 percent certain until the next morning, when his father called me during radiology rounds to congratulate me.

We finally did move into a new apartment in the art museum area and bought a row home in the same neighborhood right after we got married. By then, I was a second-year resident and Larry was in his third (and last) year of residency, so the pressure eased up a little. We had more evenings at home together when we were both awake and alert. We often went to the neighborhood gym together in the early evening and then had a late dinner at 8:30 or 9:00 before relaxing for a while and finally going to sleep. We talked a lot about the things we wanted to do "when we had time." For me, the two things that came up over and over were going to Alaska and getting a dog. One night, Larry turned to me and said, "Let's go to Alaska as soon as I'm done with this year, before I start a job. And when we get back, let's get a dog."

I named every reason why we couldn't. Because I was still in residency and I got only one week of vacation at a time. Because I still had to take call and I wouldn't be there to take care of a dog, and on and on ... But Larry was the "yes" to all my "no's." He called my chief resident and worked out a scheme for me to get two weeks off in the summer, and we explored Denali, Glacier Bay, and the Inside Passage. When we got back, we adopted a tiny black Corgi-mix puppy from the SPCA. Larry handled the dog's needs for the first year, since his new job, once residency ended, did not entail any in-hospital night call.

Larry would have loved to make all my wishes come true and shelter me from all unhappiness if he could. But some unfortunate incidents showed him how limited his power was in this regard. His first failed attempt to protect me came when our row home was burglarized. We had both been on call the same night, leaving the house empty. Larry arrived home earlier than I did the next day, as I was visiting a sick friend in the hospital. He knew this was weighing on my mind, and he also knew how badly I tended to react to things when tired, so when he came home and found the house ransacked, his first thought, after calling the police, was to try to clean it up and somehow hide the incident from me. He called his friend Lee, and the two of them set to work trying to right the house.

However, the burglars had been extremely unprofessional. They had taken little, as we had little of value; and as we learned later, a neighbor, hearing noises from the house, had called police. The police came with sirens, so the burglars ran, leaving most of the items they had intended to take. But they had spent hours in the house, drinking our liquor, eating leftover Halloween candy, and strewing the wrappers everywhere, so the house was completely taken apart. They had overturned drawers and disassembled closets. Larry and Lee could never have put everything back together in time.

When I arrived home, Lee attempted to distract me at the door, making me extremely suspicious. I pushed my way into the house to find the jumble of belongings, and Larry had to tell me the truth. Of course, I was extremely upset. It took bars on all the windows and an alarm system to make me feel safe in my home again. On the other hand, I pitched in on the cleanup effort and I helped form a neighborhood block watch to keep all our homes safe. I tried to let Larry know that reacting emotionally didn't mean I couldn't handle the problem constructively, but it was hard to tell whether he understood that.

During my third year of residency, when Larry was starting to build his academic career, I became pregnant with our first child. In medicine, there is not a "good time" in a career for a pregnancy, but this seemed like good timing for us. I would be done with residency before the baby was born, and I could set up a part-time position for the next year. The due date was admittedly awfully close to my internal medicine board exam, but if I missed the exam, I'd just have to take it the next year.

The pregnancy went along quite smoothly. Unlike many of my fellow residents who had premature contractions or other problems, I seemed healthier than ever, and with the end of residency in sight and more experience under my belt, I took in stride most of what came my way in the hospital. That is, until the night things turned nasty with one of the neurosurgery residents.

Dwayne B. had a reputation for his arrogance and brash demeanor, but I'd had very little contact with him in the hospital. This particular night, I was "house chief" in the hospital, which meant that, as a senior medical resident, I was responsible for managing all nonsurgical critical situations, assigning intensive care unit beds, and doing any emergency medical consults on surgical patients during the night. It was a busy night. There had been several "code blues" and transfers from medical floors to intensive care, and it seemed that each time one crisis was resolved, a new one presented itself.

At about 3 A.M., I entered an elevator on my way to the ICU, and there was Dwayne.

"Having a bad night?" he asked, smirking.

"Yeah, it's been one disaster after another," I replied, hoping that would be the extent of our conversation.

"Well, too bad, because I'm about to make it worse," he said. "I have a patient going for disc surgery at six A.M. He needs a medical consult."

"Why does he need a medical consult at three A.M.? Sounds routine to me; he should have gotten his consult when he came in during the day." In that era, surgical patients were generally admitted before 5:00 the day before surgery.

"I forgot to call for it. But my attending wants the consult, and the surgery's scheduled for six."

"I'm still fielding crises," I said. "I don't know if I'm going to get to it before six. It depends on how many more crashing patients I have to handle." We had exited the elevator and stood in the empty hallway, where fluorescent lights glared against the tile.

"You have to do it. It's your job. If you don't want to do your job, you should quit medicine," he told me, a nasty edge to his voice.

I took the bait. "I don't think it's your place to tell me how to do my job."

"You're such a cunt," he said quietly. "Everyone knows it. I can't believe anyone would marry you"—he looked pointedly at my pregnant belly—"much less have sex with you."

I felt as if he had slapped me. I turned and headed down the hall as fast as I could go without actually running.

I finished the consult at 5:30 because I could, and because I knew the patient shouldn't suffer for Dwayne's mistake. And because I was going to need both the neurosurgery attending and medicine attending on my side when I made my complaint.

I called Larry at 7:00. I wanted him to be upset for me, but I didn't expect him to have the reaction he did.

"I'm coming over there," he said. "I'm going to find the guy and..."

"And what, Lar?" I asked. "Punch him? That's not going to help. I'm going to take care of this on my own. You don't need to protect me."

At 8:00, I found the chief medical resident and told him about my encounter with the neurosurgery resident. He looked at me levelly and asked me what I'd done to provoke him. I wasn't all that surprised. This particular chief resident took most complaints as evidence of weakness of character. Why should this be different? By 9:00, I was sitting in the office of the residency program director and repeating my story.

"Boys will be boys," he told me. "I used to get angry when I was a resident, too."

I knew what he meant. The guy was sleep-deprived. He was under pressure. He was...but no, I couldn't give him a break on this one. He'd gone too far. He was unable to control impulses that were truly dangerous. I couldn't let him do it again to a defenseless intern or medical student or nurse, someone who might not have the guts to report him.

I made an appointment with the chairman of medicine. Before the meeting, I recorded everything I remembered in writing. After reading the account, the chairman urged me to press sexual harassment charges, but the thoughts of depositions and lawyers and courtrooms were overwhelming. All I wanted was to finish my residency in peace and have my baby. So the chairman of medicine picked up the phone and called the chairman of neurosurgery. The neurosurgery resident was put on probation and forced to write me a formal apology. I suspect this wasn't the first time he'd been abusive, and it certainly wasn't the last; I heard several months later that he'd been dismissed from the program for verbally assaulting a nurse.

It's a great fantasy scene: Larry runs in, hauls off, and slugs Dwayne. But that only happens on TV. I think there was a scene like that on *Grey's Anatomy*. Larry couldn't save me from the neurosurgical bogeyman and he certainly couldn't save me from what was about to come.

Residency finally ended in July of 1990, and I landed a part-time job in the same general medicine section as Larry. The baby was due in September. Life was beginning in earnest.

Our summer was saddened by two shocking cancer diagnoses, both in friends of our own age. One, my college roommate, died of a widespread lymphoma weeks after her diagnosis. The other, a close friend, was the first of our cohort to have breast cancer and go through chemo. Larry and I felt guilty in our luck.

Our son was born a week late by emergency C-section. Despite a long labor with some fetal distress, all seemed well at first. But a high fever kept me in the hospital, so Max stayed, too, and on the fourth night we were there, a nurse in the newborn nursery saw him turn blue. He was rushed to the neonatal ICU, where a full battery of tests revealed nothing.

We were sent home with a diagnosis of apnea. For some reason, Max occasionally went rather long periods without taking a breath during sleep. The only thing to do was to hook him up to an apnea monitor while he was sleeping so that if he didn't take a breath for 15 seconds, an alarm would go off. Then we would jostle him, which would, we hoped, get him to breathe. He would presumably grow out of this condition in a few months.

Of course, we followed the instructions for the monitor. It went off frequently at the beginning, a shrill, high-pitched beeping that made my ears ring for hours afterward. I would jump up, my heart racing, and run to the crib, only to find Max awake. It's possible that his movement caused the monitor leads to loosen and we were getting false alarms, but I actually believed that he was apneic, and that the alarm woke him up.

Sleep became an impossibility. I lay waiting. Waiting for Max to cry to nurse, waiting for the monitor, waiting for the worst. And I cried. With no sleep, soon I was crying during the day, too. Larry didn't understand it. Because in his mind, Max looked fine (and he *did,* with his blond curls and blue eyes, weighing over nine pounds at birth, nursing greedily, and growing rapidly) and the monitor was just a precaution. He knew, without a doubt, that everything would be fine.

Larry missed it. In fact, everyone, including my obstetrician at my follow-up visit, missed it. I had postpartum depression. The fact that I was still functioning, taking care of Max, doing the laundry, and planning to go back to work made it look like I was okay, maybe just a little upset about the monitor, and that reassurance would be enough. But it wasn't. My mother was the only who one realized there was a bigger problem, both because she knew me too well for my façade to fool her and because she was a trained psychologist. She came down to Philly from New Jersey and arranged child care, psychiatric care, and housekeeping.

Medication worked wonders. I was still very disturbed

about the apnea, but I could sleep and I no longer felt anxious all the time. I stopped crying. Just around that time, the monitor stopped going off at night, as well. A sleep study done at home when Max was three months old showed that his breathing pattern had improved. Not normal yet, but improved. Things were looking up.

Life was kind enough not to kick me again when I was down, but it didn't wait long. By the Christmas season, I was back at work part-time, with Max in family daycare down the street from our home. Our existence was back in a rhythm of a sort. On Christmas Eve, I went to the office to see some patients in the morning while Larry stayed home with Max. Just as I walked back into the house, the phone rang.

"Roz." My father's voice sounded strained.

"Yeah? What's wrong, Dad?"

"Your mother had a massive heart attack and..."

I remember handing the phone to Larry and sitting on the floor. The thought that "dead" was better than "on a ventilator in the ICU" was definitely in my mind, but I don't remember what I believed he was going to tell me. I only know that it was Larry who talked to my father and then laid down the phone and had to say to me, "She's dead."

And I remember hearing screaming, and that it was some time, maybe a long time, before I realized that it was coming from me, that I was sitting hunched on the floor screaming while Larry held the baby. Finally my neighbor knocked on the door to see what was wrong. That was when I stopped screaming and went on autopilot, packing bags and making calls so we could leave for New Jersey.

I think it was then that Larry finally realized that there was nothing he could do to change my world, or the way I processed it. He could get me a dog and be happy with me, and he could share in my grief, but he couldn't take it away.

By the time hepatitis C came into our lives, we'd shared plenty of grief. In my unkind moments, I'd remind Larry that the misery was primarily mine. I think this hurt him most of all.

# CHAPTER 6

# On the Wrong Side of the Curtain

O N A SUNNY morning in May of 1991, Larry and I sat in the waiting room of the clinical research unit of the Hospital of the University of Pennsylvania. We had reported to the hospital admissions office at 8 A.M. and, after filling out reams of papers, walked for what seemed like miles to get to the little-used elevator that led to the lost world called the CRU. Dark, unrenovated, and relegated to an obscure wing, the CRU, with its dull-green walls and 1960s orange vinyl chairs, was where patients in clinical trials went for experimental procedures and overnight observation. We suffered a variety of diagnoses. What we had in common was that we were desperate enough to be guinea pigs.

I had spent my two clinical years of medical school in this hospital. What I remembered were the gleaming tiled floors, fluorescent lights, and sterile supplies of the acute medical and surgical units. Medical students wore crisp white jackets as we followed attending doctors in starched, long white coats on rounds. The patients we saw had routine diagnoses, like diabetes and coronary artery disease, and the treatments they received were well-accepted recipes, delineated on the pages of Harrison's *Textbook of Internal Medicine*. I didn't know the CRU existed when I was a student. It took hepatitis C to bring me to this godforsaken place and to remove, forever, my sense of invulnerability.

Now I sat slumped in gray sweats, holding an outdated issue of *People* magazine and watching a cockroach make its way across the gray tiles of the waiting-room floor. I tried not to focus on my impending liver biopsy. Instead, I pondered the question that possessed me: How had I contracted this virus?

As a physician, I had a major risk factor. I thought about the emergency room, where I'd worked for at least six months during my residency. In that veritable bloodbath of gunshot wounds and "code blues," I'd treated hundreds of potentially infectious patients. During my first pregnancy I was called upon to put a central line (a large-bore intravenous needle, placed directly into the right side of the heart) in a patient with HIV, hepatitis B, and active tuberculosis. This was an expected part of my job, and I didn't hesitate for a second. But the reality is that I was taking a significant risk with not only my own health, but my unborn child's. At the time, I used a lot of denial to avoid facing that fact. Still, search as I might, I had no recollection of a specific needle stick or other penetrating blood or body fluid exposure.

Sexual exposure was not a likely route. But could I have

been infected with the virus through a sexual contact before I met my husband? Or perhaps there had been some kind of contamination during my cesarean section when I had my son. Again, unlikely, since I'd had no transfusions.

I wanted to be able to say the virus had been contracted in the line of duty, an explanation that sounded respectable, almost noble. I preferred it to be someone else's fault, of course, perhaps another doctor accidentally sticking me with a dirty needle during a code, or a patient suddenly thrashing and causing the needle-stick injury. I thought about the night that an angry, intoxicated patient had bitten me while I tried to put in her IV. That would have been the perfect story if not for the fact that a bite was another unlikely route of transmission. The one thing I didn't want was to be judged as someone who got sick as a result of her lifestyle choices.

No matter how I had gotten the virus, I now had to contend with it. I tortured myself with these thoughts until Dr. Payne arrived to perform my liver biopsy. He hurried into the CRU, shirttails out, holding a plastic carrier full of instruments.

"Good morning," he chirped. "All ready to go?" As if the idea of performing the biopsy cheered him.

"I guess so. Just a little anxious," I told him.

"No need for that. It's a very simple procedure."

Had he forgotten that I'd seen a number of liver biopsies performed during my training? The procedures may have been simple, but they were undeniably painful for the patient. The needles I'd seen used were very large, hollow metal tubes, about one-eighth inch in diameter with a sharp bevel, so that they left a visible hole in the skin, rather than just a tiny spot.

I had a sudden image from when I was a university student, backpacking with a friend through Europe. While in Florence, I met a young Italian man who was studying there. He served as my tour guide to the more obscure sights of the city, including a museum housing a display of instruments of torture from the Middle Ages. From my new perspective, the biopsy needle could easily have been part of that exhibit.

Dr. Payne led us to a hospital room on the unit and told me I would need to change into a gown behind a tan privacy curtain. Larry could either wait outside the room or go back to the waiting area.

"Can't he stay with me?" I pleaded. I needed Larry to hold my hand and calm me, to protect me from Dr. Payne and his needles and all the bad things that could happen to me.

"I really can't allow that," Dr. Payne replied. "This will be much easier if he waits outside."

Easier for whom? But I wasn't going to argue with him. I understood that it might make the doctor nervous to have a husband, especially a doctor-husband, scrutinizing his work. Larry went out in the hall to wait.

I pulled the curtain around the bed and changed into a flimsy, faded blue gown. Dr. Payne stood on the other side of the curtain, readying his instruments. How many times had I been on his side of the curtain? Had my patients felt as apprehensive as I did now? I remembered preparing to perform a spinal tap on a young man with signs of meningitis years ago. I needed to get it done quickly; my workday was almost over and I had a social event that evening. He was scared and kept stopping me to ask questions. I gave quick, cursory answers. If only I'd taken the time to sit down next to him and tell him what he should expect each moment, I could have made it easier. But I was focused on the test, not the patient, that day.

I opened the curtain. "Let's get this over with," I said wryly.

"First you need to sign this informed consent." Dr. Payne thrust a clipboard in my direction. "It states that you give me permission to perform a liver biopsy on you, and that you are aware of the potential complications. The complications include pneumothorax, infection, bleeding, and death."

*Death.* I had been present on numerous occasions when my patients signed such consent forms for procedures. There was always a litany of possible complications, and that list almost always included death. Being asked to sign consent for a procedure that could cause death was suddenly disorienting, like looking at a word you've known all your life and suddenly feeling that the spelling is wrong. I grabbed the pen and scrawled an illegible signature.

I followed Dr. Payne's instructions to lie on my back and pull up my gown to expose my ribs on the right. He sterilized the area with Betadine solution and put a sterile paper drape with a hole in the center over me. He put on sterile gloves and poked around at my ribs. Next, he took a syringe full of local anesthetic and injected the skin. Pinpricks didn't bother me much. Then he picked up the biopsy needle, and I closed my eyes.

"Okay, when I say to take a breath, I want you to breathe in and hold it. You can't move at all until I'm done."

"Okay," I said. Infection, bleeding, and death. What was okay about this?

"Take a breath."

I took a deep breath. I held it. I kept my eyes closed. I felt a hard punch to my ribs, but I didn't move.

"Okay, you can breathe."

I opened my eyes and saw him staring into the bloodied biopsy needle.

"Damn, not enough tissue!" he exclaimed. "I'm going to have to try again. This time you have to be completely still."

I knew I'd been completely still, but I couldn't say anything. We'd come this far. I was going to have to let him do it again. My right side ached. I nodded, but tears were dripping down my face.

Dr. Payne looked annoyed. I had provided inadequate tissue and now I was crying. I guess he was frustrated.

"Ready? Take a breath."

I closed my eyes and took another breath. This time, the blow was sharper and more intense. In a few seconds a deep, but not unbearable, pain settled in my right shoulder.

I opened my eyes. Dr. Payne seemed satisfied. The needle was filled with gelatinous brown stuff that looked like raw calves' liver. He told me to turn on my right side, and that I would have to lie in that position for two hours. Then he left, sending Larry in from the hall.

The rest of the day went by in a blur. Larry sat with me for a while. I didn't feel like talking, and there was nothing to say. I was relieved, but felt physically battered and emotionally exhausted. Soon Larry left for work. I couldn't read lying on my side. There was no TV and no phone. I lay there, staring at the cracked wall and wishing for sleep, which didn't come. By mid-afternoon I was allowed to sit up, and a friend came to visit.

We made jokes about the décor and avoided talking about the biopsy.

In the evening, Larry came back, Max in tow. Someone had given Max a red balloon and he was running up and down the hallway with it. I was allowed to get up and walk in the hall, but I didn't have the energy to chase after a toddler. Larry took him home to bed.

I tried to rest, but at midnight, a college-age girl checked into the unit for some kind of monthly infusion and was placed in the other bed in my room. She clearly had done this many times before and did not let her medical issues hamper her social life; she started talking loudly on the phone as soon as she got settled in, and her conversation went on and on. By 1 A.M., I'd had it, but I wasn't feeling very assertive, so instead of confronting my roommate, I went out to the nurses' station to ask for assistance.

"Oh, she's here a lot," the portly male night nurse told me. "I don't want to tell her to hang up. I'll find another spot for you." He sighed, put down his paperback, and hauled himself out of his chair. He showed me to another room with only one bed, unoccupied. I climbed in and turned out the light. I spent a fitful few hours in bed, and finally got up at 6 A.M., feeling irritable and tired but pain-free. I begged the nurse to get me discharged. He seemed happy to see me go. I was not one of his regulars and had disturbed his night. I refused a wheelchair and walked to the front of the hospital to hail a cab. The cabbie spoke little English and drove up the expressway at 75 miles an hour. By the time I got home, Larry had taken Max to the babysitter and gone to work. I got into my own bed and fell asleep.

A week passed after the biopsy, and then a second week. Dr Payne had promised results within 10 days, but I was afraid to call and ask for them. I desperately wanted to know how much liver disease I had but was equally desperate to stay in my state of limbo, where I didn't have to consider the next step. Finally, after two weeks had passed, I asked Larry to call for results.

"You really should call your doctor yourself," Larry said. "He's not allowed to give me your results."

"I can't. I'm afraid of him. Please do it for me," I begged.

"Okay, I'll try."

*Afraid of my doctor.* It sounds so ridiculous, so immature. Little children are sometimes afraid of the pediatrician, and my dogs show fear when they see the veterinarian; small children and animals don't understand why they have to be subjected to uncomfortable exams or procedures. My position, as a medically sophisticated adult, cannot be compared to theirs. I knew this was all for my own benefit, after all. The doctor had only my best interest at heart.

Or did he? Perhaps part of my trepidation had to do with a deep-seated belief that Dr. Payne really didn't care about me. For one thing, we'd never really connected. In my professional life, I knew what connection felt like to the physician. It helped me do my best work; it made me care. Since I didn't feel connected to Dr. Payne, I assumed he didn't feel it either, and that made it hard for me to believe in his caring.

Perhaps a more tangible concern was the fact that Dr. Payne's role was not simply to be my doctor. If I needed treatment and met the criteria, I would be enrolled in his interferon study. He would be both my doctor and a clinical investigator, and I would be both patient and subject. In the ideal world, it would all fall into place. I would benefit from the treatment, and he would have the benefit of positive data to report. Then other patients would benefit from the data. But in reality, I might not meet the treatment criteria, or the treatment might not work, or some side effect might force Dr. Payne to consider removing me from the protocol. These situations could present a conflict of interest if what was best for me was not best for the data. Ethically, Dr. Payne had to choose my well-being over his data, but how could I be sure he would?

This was not the first time I'd been a study subject, so I knew the pitfalls. As a medical student, I'd volunteered for a study of a vaccine for chicken pox. I was hoping to benefit by gaining immunity to chicken pox, and the investigators were hoping to determine the correct dose of vaccine for an adult. Unfortunately, I received a dose too low to confer full immunity, and the protocol did not provide for a booster. They got useful data and were done with me, but I got questionable benefit (though later, I was exposed to the disease and didn't get it, so my partial immunity turned out to be enough).

I'd also been a clinical investigator, so I knew that perspective as well. My study, which I conducted during medical school, involved interviewing pregnant adolescents and their mothers, trying to determine how maternal attitudes affected adolescent contraceptive practices. The subjects volunteered in exchange for a small payment. I wasn't required to treat them in any way. But certainly, there were emotional consequences to being interviewed. While I was sensitive to this fact, and didn't want to upset my subjects, my primary goal was to collect the data, so I tried to always complete the interview, even if the subject was distressed.

That's the nature of research; the loyalty is partly to the research itself. So how could I feel completely safe? I wasn't Dr. Payne's only concern in our relationship. Maybe I wasn't even his primary concern.

Because of our tenuous relationship, and the fear of the biopsy result itself, I honestly was afraid to make that phone call.

Later that day, Larry called me with the results. My doctor, with no consideration for my confidentiality, had freely given Larry the information, in what I imagined was a man-to-man, paternalistic delivery. I'm sure it was easier for Dr. Payne that way, since the news wasn't particularly good.

"He says you have moderate inflammation, no scarring, but enough going on that he thinks you should get treated," Larry reported.

I still don't know what I was expecting. I should have been relieved by the news that I had no scarring, but instead I was devastated. I guess I was holding out hope that I would be told the disease was so insignificant that I could forget about it and get on with my life. I burst into tears. Larry tried to console me, but it was futile, so we ended our phone call. I decided to call Dr. Payne to find out what I was supposed to do next.

Hearing the distress in my voice, Dr. Payne told me that he wasn't sure I should be treated after all. "You know, the interferon can make you depressed. I'm not sure you should take it if you're not emotionally stable."

"What are you talking about?" I asked. "This isn't depression! I'm upset about the biopsy results. I can handle the treatment."

Suddenly, I was in the position of convincing my doctor to give me treatment that only minutes ago I'd been hoping not to get! Everything was upside down and backwards. But I'd gotten the message loud and clear: I would never again risk being honest about my feelings with Dr. Payne.

"Okay, we'll get you on the treatment protocol," he told me. "But why don't we start it in September? No reason to rush into things. Enjoy your summer, and I'll mail you a prescription at the end of August. You can get started and then we'll have a follow-up appointment."

I agreed half-heartedly and we hung up. I was not pleased with the plan. If I needed treatment, I wanted to get it and be done, but I'd lost my nerve. I was at the mercy of Dr. Payne and his experimental protocol, a world in which he was the "principal investigator" who would assign me a random number. I was officially a guinea pig.

# CHAPTER 7

# How Did I Get It?: The Stigma of Hepatitis C

D URING MY "HEPATITIS Years," I spent a lot of time wondering where my infection came from. It was a waste of time. I would never know for sure. My best guess, as I said before, was patient care, most likely in the emergency room. Things there moved fast and furious, and there were so many more blood exposures than on the hospital floors or in the outpatient clinics. I, like my colleagues, didn't report every minor breach of the "universal precautions" that were supposed to be followed—I ignored a few tiny, superficial needle sticks and blood splashes from patients who were deemed "low risk." What we were really worried about was HIV. We'd all been vaccinated for hepatitis B, and we didn't really know about hepatitis C during my medical school and most of my residency years. But in restrospect, how would anyone know who was "high risk" or "low risk"? Look at me.

Unless you knew I had hepatitis C, I would have clearly been deemed "low risk."

I didn't have any of the official risk factors—intravenous drug use or transfusions before 1992. Contamination during my C-section was highly unlikely. Exposure from sexual activity before marriage in 1988 was even more remote a possibility. But truly, I will never know for sure.

The saving grace for us, as physicians, is that we can say that our infections came from occupational exposures. Even if we don't say it explicitly, it is assumed by our doctors, our friends, and our families. In essence, people have sympathy for us. This is exactly what I was thinking about my own illness: I wanted it to be from my patient care and not from my lifestyle.

But why should that matter? A virus is a virus, isn't it? Who has the right to judge according to how the virus got into my bloodstream? I feared being judged by others, but obviously, I was also judging myself. And I, of all people, should have known better. As a physician who trained in the era of HIV, I had no excuse for being ignorant or prejudiced about such matters. And yet, here I was, having these thoughts.

What difference does it make where an infection comes from? It is the same virus, the same infection, whether it came from a medical needle, a drug needle, or transfusion blood. We are all in the same unfortunate position of having hepatitis C. Should I be treated with more dignity, more empathy, than someone who got the virus in a different manner than I?

We doctors, like every other patient, are afraid of being stigmatized by our disease. We are afraid that others, out of ignorance, will want to avoid us, will be afraid of our touch, be afraid of sharing towels or dishes or glasses with us, when truly they only need to avoid our blood (as they should avoid anyone's blood, really). Yet we stigmatize our patients, making them feel dirty and worthless. Healthcare workers may show impatience, make negative comments, and show displeasure at drawing blood from patients with hepatitis C, particularly if those patients are IV drug abusers. Those in healthcare should be the most sensitive to the stigma that a blood-borne disease like hepatitis C carries. Studies show that patients who are stigmatized by the healthcare system are significantly more likely to decrease health-seeking behavior. Nevertheless, we continue to stigmatize patients even now. Recent reports show that more than 50 percent of hep C patients report alienation in medical care, feeling that they are seen as inferior, bad, or "dirty" because of their infections. Patients with hepatitis C who are perceived to have contracted the disease from drug use, those who are female, and those who are Hispanic experience more humiliation in their medical treatment, leading to increased levels of anxiety and depression and poorer quality of life. It seems that people who already feel ashamed of their diagnoses are becoming even more isolated and disenfranchised.

It is not only the medical world that has negative attitudes toward hepatitis C patients, but society in general, in the United States and in Europe. Obviously, not enough has been done to educate the public about this disease. Back in the early 1990s, when I had the virus, there was essentially no such education.

Of course, we can't completely change how we feel. However, we can be more aware of our feelings and try to educate ourselves about stigma and our resulting behavior toward our patients.

There are certainly deep roots and controversies to some of the stigma. For instance, does one view IV drug abuse as an illness in itself or as a lifestyle choice? I personally would argue that it's an illness, but I know many people don't agree with me.

Digging deeper, being a doctor is a lifestyle choice, too. Doesn't that make doctors "responsible" for their own disease, especially if a needle-stick exposure occurred because of carelessness during a procedure or failure to adhere to universal precautions? I can certainly think back to moments during a procedure when I regretted a tiny misstep such as attempting to put a cap back on a used needle, which puts the doctor at risk of sticking herself, rather than throwing it directly into the "sharps" container, though I knew this was wrong. I'm fairly sure other doctors, especially doctors-in-training, make such errors and wish they hadn't. But we can't take them back. What's done is done.

So is the issue whether a patient is "responsible" for his disease? We certainly don't choose our disease. Yet most doctors, IV drug abusers, and even patients receiving transfusions are well aware of the risks of their behaviors. It's just that once we have reached a certain point in our life paths, we don't have the control we might ideally hope for over our behavior. The transfusion patient needs that blood. The doctor must perform that risky procedure. The IV drug user needs that fix.

Then maybe it's not so much "responsibility" as "blame" that contributes to the stigma. Are we to blame for having hepatitis C? Do we deserve it? This question has been explored in detail regarding HIV. There are those who believe that HIV is punishment for homosexuality or other "undesirable" behavior.

So could hepatitis C be a punishment for "living wrong," also? Most people, when asked such a question, would say, "Of course not!" Yet for those with chronic or terminal illnesses of all types, but perhaps most notably with those diseases that are blood-borne and/or associated with lifestyle choices, these questions are not so easily put to rest.

Even if the "rational" answer is that such a disease does not make one "bad" or "dirty," I don't know many infected people for whom these question have not lingered and nagged. I suppose it is part of exploring the meaning of being ill. It is the dark side of the exploration, as compared to finding a silver lining, such as living each day to its fullest or reconnecting with loved ones, that illness may bring.

I knew realistically that my disease was not my fault. I didn't truly believe that I deserved it. I did ask myself many times, though, "Why me?" Not in the self-pitying way that it sounds. I wasn't so much questioning the fairness of the universe as wondering whether perhaps I'd actually done something wrong, something that made this happen. If in some way I did deserve to have hepatitis C. This line of thinking made little sense. That's exactly how we stigmatize ourselves.

Also, regardless of my education and all my understanding of the mechanisms of infection, I worried that I would infect others I cared about. This also made little sense. Finally, I worried that my patients or even my friends wouldn't want me near them if they knew. Some of the latter concern may have been valid, had I tested it out. Fear and ignorance are common, and hepatitis C was, after all, a new disease that people knew little about at the time, in 1991.

I had very few people with whom to discuss my situation. As a physician with hep C, I felt very isolated. There had to be others like me out there, but I didn't know any of them. Just how many doctors are there who have been infected? I've looked for the data and can't find it. Studies vary greatly on estimates of how much more common hepatitis C is in healthcare workers than in the general population. Most agree that it is at least somewhat more common, maybe up to three times so.

Even data on rates of infection in healthcare workers exposed to hepatitis C from accidental needle-stick injuries vary greatly from study to study. There are studies that followed exposed healthcare workers for a year and showed no infections, and some that showed rates as high as 10 percent. This great variation most likely has to do with the fact that deep sticks with large amounts of blood in larger-bore needles, such as the kind used in trauma surgery, are much riskier than superficial sticks with smaller needles. Blood from patients with more virus in their blood is also more infectious.

I guess it's not that surprising that I haven't come upon many doctors with hep C. It's not something that would be freely discussed or disclosed. If physicians are tested for blood-borne disease like hep C or HIV, it is voluntarily. The only doctors felt to pose potential harm to their patients if they are infected are surgeons who do surgeries deep in body cavities, during which the potential for scalpels going through gloves is high. Examples are trauma surgery and cardiothoracic surgery. Still, testing is voluntary. A positive test would end the career that a physician has trained for over many years, and into which he has put his heart and soul.

I did speak to one other doctor with hep C about a year into my ordeal. My internist had me make contact with her, and I think he did this believing we might provide support for each other. I was junior faculty, and in Dr. Payne's first interferon protocol. I guess I was handling it fairly well at the time. The other doctor was in her last year of residency; I don't remember what specialty. But when I spoke to her on the phone, she was doing much worse than I. She had more severe liver disease than I did and was very depressed. She was not hopeful about the interferon. I found myself in the role of counselor and comforter to her, a role I couldn't afford to take on. I felt more demoralized about my own disease after the conversation. We didn't speak again.

I imagine this kind of scenario happens all the time when patients talk to each other: the people or group might bring wonderful support, but the wrong person at the wrong time might only deepen one's sense of isolation.

If only the right person had been there, I wonder what it would have been like. I try to imagine now what relief I would have felt if there'd been someone else who was really in the same boat—another doctor or a nurse, maybe, getting the same treatment. Someone who was doing all right. We could have encouraged each other and listened to each other and complained to each other, like friends. I really wish I'd had that.

# CHAPTER 8

# The Outsider

L ATE AUGUST, 1991, the Outer Banks of North Carolina. I sat on a white plastic chaise on the deck of the enormous beachfront house we'd rented, with three other families, for a week. Books and papers were spread on the chaise next to me, as I tried to study for my impending internal medicine board examination. I sat alone on the deck, for it was early afternoon, the sun and humid North Carolina heat at their peaks. The children were napping and the other adults sat in the air-conditioned living room, chatting or reading the newspaper. Occasional laughter floated out to me through the sliding glass doors.

Nobody else had brought any work on this vacation. Larry and the other physician couple in our group, Lee and Cathy, had passed their boards two years earlier, and their jobs did not require much work outside the office. Our other companions were Neil and Leslie, both in business, and John and Barbara, a lawyer and speech therapist, respectively. They'd all planned on a work-free week. So there I was, in the only place I was guaranteed not to be disturbed.

Unfortunately, my concentration was not good, despite the quiet and solitude. The board exam was set for late September. I got a knot in my stomach just thinking about how much I needed to commit to memory before then. I briefly wondered whether our row home in Philadelphia, with its aptly jaundice-yellow kitchen, would ever be sold. We'd had it on the market for six months, without any serious offers. We needed more space, with our son, and we'd experienced way too much personal crime in our neighborhood—not only had our home been burglarized, but our car had been broken into. Maybe we'd be stuck in that house forever. That idea made me anxious, too. But why worry about that, when I was supposed to start interferon as soon as our vacation was over?

In case it isn't obvious, I was feeling a bit sorry for myself on this particular day. It started with the "Why me?" thoughts. Why was I stuck studying on vacation while everyone else relaxed? Why couldn't I sit around the table telling stories with my friends after dinner, instead of excusing myself to study? Then again, I wouldn't be much fun, since they were all drinking wine, and I couldn't do that either. Alcohol would put more stress on my liver. They were all so lucky to be healthy and carefree. Nobody seemed to notice—not even my own husband—that I was on the outside of it all.

I didn't want to dwell on the fact that Larry didn't notice, because that made me angry. At the beginning of this hepatitis C ordeal, when we used to talk about it relatively often, he'd tell me, "We'll go through this together. You won't be alone in it." But I *was* alone. I would continue to be alone. He could give lip service to the problem being "our problem," but the facts were obvious. It was my disease; it was my body; it was my problem.

When everyone else went home from this vacation, their lives would go on as usual. I would go home and face a month of cramming for boards in our crowded row home, while also injecting toxic chemicals into my body, which would make me sick as a dog. This wasn't my first illness; I'd lived through several others, including some with hospitalization, the first when I was very young. Though my memory of other events from early childhood wasn't always clear, I remembered that episode in excruciating detail, as I did other physical traumas.

*I am four years old. My father carries me up the stairs. My head throbs unbearably with each step he takes. I am too tired to cry. He tucks me into bed in my cotton knit pajamas with the feet, the pale yellow ones with the pom-pom at the neck. Later, I wake in the dark to the sound of my father's voice. He carries me back downstairs to the family room, my head pounding, my skin on fire. The pediatrician sits on the brown quilted sofa, and my father places me next to him. The doctor shines a light in my eyes, and I draw back in pain. Then he asks me to touch my chin to my bent knee. I try; I always try to please. But my neck hurts too much, and I can't. The doctor says something to my parents.*

*I am wrapped in a blanket and carried to the car. Then I am on a high bed on wheels, facing a dull-green tiled wall. Someone tells me to stay still, and there is a sharp pain in my low back as a needle is inserted. The nurse says they are doing a test to find out why my head hurts so much. She says I have to stay in the hospital, and my mother promises to stay with me.*

*I wake much later in a hospital room. It is sunny and I am alone. I scream for my mother. Moments later she appears.*

*"Here I am! It's okay. I'm right here. You were asleep and I just went to the bathroom. I've been right here all night," she tells me, gesturing at the orange vinyl chair next to my bed.*

*Each night, I wake up and scream until one of my parents comes back to the hospital. I scream when they take me to X-ray. They take the pom-pom from my pajamas because it interferes with the films.*

*I am discharged after a week. I feel fine, but I am not allowed to play outside or to walk barefoot on the floor, since my parents are afraid I will get sick again. Since I'm not allowed to walk on the tile floor, I walk around on the furniture, thinking I am very clever. I remain afraid of the pediatrician for the rest of my childhood.*

*Years later, my mother tells me that she read that children who have meningitis become mentally retarded, and she was terrified that I would never be the same.*

*I am 14. I have golf-ball-size swollen lymph nodes in the front of my neck. My father takes me to the doctor. He says I need blood tests. My parents seem worried, but they tell me everything will be fine. A few days later, the doctor calls, just at the beginning of our Passover seder. My father talks to him; I hear my father laughing loudly. I ask him what's so funny. He*

*says nothing is funny; the doctor says I have mononucleosis.*
*I will probably get a fever and sore throat soon. Later, my*
*mother tells me he was laughing because he was relieved.*
*The doctor had thought I had lymphoma. He is ecstatic that*
*it turned out to just be mono.*

*Two days later, I have a temperature of 103 and the worst*
*sore throat of my life. I can't swallow. This lasts for over a*
*week, and I drift in and out of a delirious sleep. I stay home*
*from school, but I mostly take care of myself, since my par-*
*ents are both working. It's just mono; I'll be fine. People from*
*the Jehovah's Witness church come to the door one day while*
*I'm home sick and I tell them they can't come in because I*
*have a contagious illness. I think this is ironic.*

*Soon I go back to school. Everything goes back to nor-*
*mal, but my lymph nodes stay swollen for months, and after*
*that, they swell dramatically every time I get a cold.*

*I am 16. I have two swollen finger joints. My doctor has no*
*idea what to make of them. He sends me to an orthopedic*
*surgeon, who says I have cysts in my joints and need sur-*
*gery. A few weeks later he removes the cysts, but when I go*
*back to have the stitches out he tells me they were not cysts,*
*but rheumatoid nodules, evidence that I have rheumatoid*
*arthritis. He sends me to a rheumatologist, who draws eight*
*vials of blood. At a follow-up visit, he tells me and my par-*
*ents that there is no way to tell whether I will have severe*
*arthritis over the next few years or have a mild course.*
*None of my bloodwork has come back abnormal, but that*
*guarantees nothing.*

*I go to the library and read about rheumatoid arthritis, then cry for days, believing I will become disabled and live in terrible pain. Months pass, my fingers heal, and no other joints swell or hurt. After a while, I decide to forget about it. Nothing ever happens to my joints.*

*I am 20, a junior in college, living in Boston for the summer while I work in a lab and study for my Medical College Admissions Test. My eye is red and itchy one day, then it hurts. I go to my roommate's eye doctor and he gives me eyedrops, but the next day it feels worse, and I have a fever. My vision is blurry, so I call the eye doctor back. He tells me to go to Massachusetts Eye and Ear Hospital for a culture. The young doctor there tells me it is not pink eye; I have a rip-roaring viral infection of my cornea. I end up in the hospital for a week. I have to use eyedrops every two hours and take antibiotics so I don't lose the vision in that eye.*

*I don't feel well for over a month after that. My parents are worried and make me come home for the rest of the summer. Nobody can figure out why I got so sick from an eye infection. I have minor recurrences every couple of months for the next year or so, and then very occasionally for many years after. My eye tears abnormally even after the infection clears, and it will for the rest of my life.*

*I am 25, in my last year of medical school. I have frequent stomachaches and start having bloody bowel movements. I go to Student Health and the nurse-practitioner there sends me to a gastroenterologist, who does a sigmoidoscopy.*

*He tells me I probably have ulcerative colitis. I take medicine for it, but it doesn't get better for months. Then it is gone as quickly as it came. But a few months into my internship it returns, more severe, and I have so much abdominal pain it is hard to work. I see one of the GI docs, and he insists I have a colonoscopy. Again, I am told I have ulcerative colitis. I take different medications, and after a few months I have no symptoms. I stop the medication but worry a lot, because I know ulcerative colitis can get much more severe, and that some patients have courses requiring hospitalization and even surgery. Mysteriously, I have never had similar symptoms again, and another colonoscopy two years later is completely normal. I tell my parents very little about this because they worry too much. After the second colonoscopy, I tell them it was all a mistake and I don't have it after all. The doctors aren't sure whether I actually have anything chronic.*

The medical problems I had over the years all resolved or at least remitted. I did not have leukemia or a brain tumor, or even bad chronic asthma. Everything that happened to me was temporary, but some of these illnesses weren't quite ordinary. They were just a little scary, a little dramatic. If they didn't frighten me, they certainly frightened my parents.

After the meningitis, my father treated me differently. I was not to become a tough little kid, climbing trees and riding my bike at top speed. I was, in his eyes, fragile, a china doll. He even called me "doll" or "dolly" or "*mausela*" (Yiddish for "little mouse"), a confirmation of my smallness, my breakable nature.

He worried constantly about my health, always watching for signs of a cold or other illness. He kept a bottle of vile cough syrup called Terpin Hydrate (for obvious reasons, I misunderstood and called it "Turpentine" until I was much older) and pulled it out at the first tiny cough. In my child's mind, it was punishment for getting sick, but I think he believed if he could suppress the symptoms immediately, he could keep me well.

The mono and rheumatoid illness in my teens further proved my sickly constitution. As I got older, I joked with my father that he was a hypochondriac, but instead of worrying about himself, he worried about me. I knew that it was his way of caring. He couldn't bear the thought of something happening to me, and it made my health a touchy topic. I was always trying to prove I was healthy and strong, and he was always showing me evidence that I wasn't. He hated my penchant for risky physical activity like skiing and climbing. Before my internship started, I planned to go on a whitewater rafting trip in the Colorado wilderness. My father panicked when he asked how he could reach me by phone and I told him he couldn't. I know he spent the ten days of my trip holding his breath, waiting for me to call saying I was still alive. Though I came back from the trip with more confidence in my body, feeling healthy and strong, my father did not accept the trip as proof of my health, but rather proof of my foolishness.

There was not much room for my mother in our disagreement about my physical well-being. This was just as well, since she was engaged in a similar battle with my brother over his mental health and lifestyle, also an ongoing issue since childhood. He struggled with moodiness and attention deficit problems.

He was brilliant and musically extremely talented, and had a fine academic career, attending MIT for his PhD and landing a tenured professorship in his 20s, but was a constant source of concern for my parents, as he continued into adulthood to be frighteningly disorganized and socially unhappy. Emotional life was my mother's bailiwick, one my father was afraid of, so they divided, if not conquered, their children's problems.

After my mother died, my father was on his own and tried to fill in for my mother, but his self-assigned tasks were too large for him as he aged. He had lengthy phone conversations with my brother and listened, but had no advice to offer. He still asked frequently after my health and often commented that I was too thin, or looked tired or pale, but no longer pushed vitamins or medications on me.

My diagnosis with hepatitis C was, to my father, the final confirmation of what he had known about me all along. He listened to the information I gave him with concern and tried to reassure me, but was himself pessimistic about the prognosis. I found myself leaving out a lot, feeling that it was better for both of us if he knew few details of my illness and treatment. He rarely brought the topic up, as though he were afraid that reminding me would make it worse (as if I could forget). In the months after my diagnosis, my father became progressively more frail and, eventually, ill himself, developing a rare form of dementia. The tables were turned, and I was taking care of him. He still asked how I was feeling every time I spoke to him. More and more, I needed to tell him I was fine, and he needed to believe it.

When I needed a little of the sympathy that my father had provided, I could still turn to my brother, who took over the role of worrying about me. He was always willing to listen, even to the gory details, and was steadfastly empathetic and caring. Yet accepting his support worried me; he worried too much, and I saw him, perhaps inaccurately, as being too fragile to deal with my problems as well as his own. I didn't like to burden him too frequently. I also didn't want him to take over my father's view of me as an invalid.

*Invalid* is a powerful word. To be an invalid is to be seen as not valid, as less than others. Perhaps I wanted some sympathy, but I did not want—even now, as I contemplated starting treatment with interferon—to be viewed as an invalid. Still, here I was, moping about and behaving like a hermit on this vacation.

What was this about? I'd been here, the sick person among the well, before. But all the temporary illnesses, no matter how severe, had not prepared me for the separateness I felt as a person with a serious chronic illness. I was no longer part of the carefree world of the well, and it was clear to me that most of my family, friends, and colleagues understood little of the new world I had entered.

Looking back, I see that I chose to maintain my isolation, believing it was the safest thing to do. I hadn't yet learned to trust others to try to comprehend my plight, nor had I learned to accept less than complete understanding. And at that time, I still believed strongly in pride, in the value of saving face and proving the ability to go it alone. The fact that I was only a year out of residency didn't help that. And it was what I'd always done. In proving to my family that I was okay after each illness, I had pushed myself and coped, no matter how difficult it was. I didn't take time off when I didn't feel well. I tried not to complain, for fear there would be some consequence (remember the Terpin Hydrate?).

In fact, this self-management was probably what led to my choice to go into medicine. I remember thinking when I had mono, at 14, that the whole thing was very interesting. I looked up information about the virus and learned how little there was to be done once it was diagnosed, other than to wait it out. The way the germ worked fascinated me. But more fascinating was the way it made me feel, not so much physically, but in the world, as this separate being for whom time and activity had to stop for a certain period until, magically, one day, I was able to function again. And then how my functioning wasn't the same as it had been before, and how I had to accommodate the change. After the rheumatoid nodules and my eye disease, I had quite a bit of experience with being altered, vulnerable, and yet strangely resilient. Who better than I to guide someone else to wholeness after such a trauma? Of course, it would be much later that I would start teaching my patients to reach out for support.

I could have marched back into the house and talked to my husband and my friends, my supposedly close friends. Lee was heavily into holistic health and the previous year had inflicted on all of us his plan of ultra-low-fat heart-healthy cooking and meditation. I could have put him to work cooking liver-detoxifying dinners for me. And since three of my housemates had passed the board exam, I could have asked for help studying, or we could have played quiz games, so I didn't have to sit alone with my books. I could have talked to Cathy and Barbara and Leslie about my worries about mothering my child while on interferon. We might have ended up closer at the end of the week. But instead, I left them to their world and retreated to mine, creating a chasm out of the ordinary space between us.

Larry opened the sliding glass door.

"The kids are all up. We're going in the pool, if you want to join us. Max is asking for you."

I looked down at my books. I'd covered only one of the three sections I had planned to cover that afternoon. I'd have to do extra the next day. I got up and put the books away.

That evening, I watched Cathy nursing her infant son. They looked utterly peaceful, as though nothing could harm them. I wondered what it felt like to be that secure. If I had another baby, I would never feel that we were untouchable. Anything could happen. If my treatment didn't work, I'd have to worry that, if I got pregnant, I would pass the hep C to the baby. And as for nursing, nobody knew whether the virus could be passed through breast milk.

The last day of our vacation, I sat again on the deck, alone. I was at least three days behind in my studying. The facts just weren't sticking. I was ordinarily a very efficient student, with good study habits and excellent retention of information. All the tumult in my life was distracting me.

I heard the phone ring inside. A few minutes later, Larry came out to the deck, a big smile on his face.

"Guess what?" he asked.

"What?"

"We have an offer on the house! It's five thousand less than we were asking, but the guy already has a mortgage commitment and there's no contingency!"

"That's great!" For a moment I felt light, elated. "Let's take it!" I jumped up from my deck chair and threw my arms around him.

"That's what I thought you'd say," he said, laughing. "I'm going in to call the Realtor right now." He kissed me on the head and deposited me back in my chair.

The moment faded to my background anxiety pretty quickly. Yes, this was finally some good news. One less long-term problem. But that meant we'd have to start packing. Was this going to be too much for me?

*Ugh,* I thought to myself, *you have got to stop thinking so negatively! Get over it and do what you need to do!*

I returned to my books and forced myself to learn a mnemonic.

We arrived home after a nine-hour drive the next evening. A box of mail sat in the living room, collected by our next-door neighbor while we were away. Among the catalogs and bills was an envelope from the Division of Gastroenterology and Liver Diseases at the Hospital of the University of Pennsylvania. Inside was the prescription for my alpha interferon.

# CHAPTER 9

# Doctors Make the Worst Patients

I LAID OUT MY array of equipment, ready to inject my first dose of interferon alpha-2b. I had a vial of clear liquid. It looked innocuous enough, like water. I had alcohol swabs, syringes that held up to three milliliters (cc's), and two types of needles: one relatively large, to draw up the medication, and the other shorter and fine-bored, to inject myself. My favorite new possession, however, was my red plastic needle disposal container adorned with a skull-and-crossbones sticker.

The pharmacist had supplied me, in addition, with an instruction sheet for drawing up and injecting the interferon. Later, I would find out that other patients had several scheduled sessions with a nurse at Dr. Payne's office to learn the proper injection technique, review side effects, and receive answers to any questions on medication administration. Apparently, my physician status had exempted me from these visits; they were not even offered to me.

The assumption that I would know how to perform a subcutaneous injection was erroneous; this was something nurses did and doctors usually did not do. Even if I did know how, injecting oneself is completely different from injecting someone else. Damned if I was going to tell anyone I needed help, though. I didn't even mention it to Larry. When I finally asked him for help months later, it turned out that he did know how to give a proper subcutaneous injection. But I was determined to be independent about this. Obviously, I was "supposed" to know how, or someone would have offered to show me. So here I was, learning from an instruction sheet.

I wiped the top of the vial with alcohol and picked up a syringe, with the larger needle attached. I drew up half a cc and tapped the air out of the syringe. I changed the needle to the smaller one. Then I wiped the front of my thigh with alcohol. So far, so good. I uncapped the small needle.

The instructions simply said to inject subcutaneously into the anterior thigh. I didn't know what the angle of the needle should be or how quickly to inject. Knowing that subcutaneous meant rather superficial, I stabbed the needle in at a 45-degree angle. Then I pushed down on the plunger. Ouch! There was a lot of pressure and burning. I pulled out the needle when the syringe was empty and tossed it into the disposal container. A purple bruise was already forming on my thigh. No bleeding, though. I figured I'd done okay.

I sat and waited for something to happen. It was nighttime, as I'd been told to give myself the injections three times weekly at bedtime. I got in bed and turned on the TV. I watched a police drama. By the end, still nothing had happened. I turned out the light and went to sleep.

The next morning, I woke to Larry's voice. "Time to get up. Max is already up and dressed."

Larry was fully dressed for work. I felt very far away and foggy. As I became more alert, I noted a dull headache. My body felt achy, too, as though I'd exercised too hard. I dragged myself from bed, thinking a shower would make me feel better, but after my shower, I just wanted to go back to bed. Unfortunately, it was Tuesday, and I had a full day of work ahead of me. *Okay,* I thought. *This isn't so bad. It might have been a lot worse. I can definitely function feeling this way.*

I took some Tylenol and got dressed. I went through the usual routine of getting breakfast for Max and taking him to daycare. The drive to work was a blur, and I arrived feeling exhausted, but the headache was gone. The day went on as though nothing were different. I decided it would be tolerable for the six months and felt tremendously relieved.

That night, there was no shot, and Wednesday I felt back to my usual self. I took another shot Wednesday night, and I had the same low-grade headache and body aches on Thursday. In addition, I noticed that I had very little appetite. By 3 P.M. my stomach hurt a little, and when I got home at 5:00, having picked up Max at daycare and carted him and his little backpack home, I had intense abdominal cramps. I settled Max with some toys on the bedroom floor and went into the bathroom. After ten minutes of violent diarrhea, I felt better, though I was exhausted. I didn't go with Larry and Max and Ubu to the dog park that evening. Instead, I lay on the bed, wondering whether this was supposed to happen with the interferon. I got out the package insert from the vial and read it. No mention was made of abdominal pain or diarrhea. I decided it had been a coincidence.

The cycle went on: shots on Monday, Wednesday, and Friday; side effects on Tuesday, Thursday, and Saturday. Sundays were my day off, the one day in the week with no shot and no headache or body pain. Most of my "side effect" days also included belly pain and diarrhea, and I lost ten pounds in the first six weeks of treatment. I called Dr. Payne to ask what to do, but he told me it wasn't an interferon side effect. I couldn't decide whether he was wrong or I was crazy. Despite these problems, I was pleased that I could manage.

After a month of interferon injections, I had my blood drawn to see whether my liver function tests had improved. Normalization of liver enzymes would make me a "responder," increasing my chances of long-term benefit from the medication to about 50 percent. Rather than go to Dr. Payne's office and then wait for him to call me with results, I had the blood drawn at my own office and received the results myself the next day. The liver function tests were normal! My first hurdle had been jumped, and I had a reason to keep going.

This is not to say that there were no bumps in the road. The first major bump was self-induced, fueled by my anxiety and fear. I had continued to inject myself as I had the first night, with the needle at a 45-degree angle, and I had bruises all over my thighs. I started thinking about the bruising. I had seen many patients who got subcutaneous injections and never heard them complain about bruising. Why was I all black and blue?

Maybe something was wrong with my blood-clotting mechanisms. After all, the liver makes clotting factors, and I had liver disease. But only advanced, severe liver disease would cause clotting problems, and everyone said my liver should be working fine. Well, I decided to check my clotting anyway, and had the two standard tests, the protime (PT) and partial thromboplastin time (PTT), drawn. The results came back to me the same afternoon. The PT was very elevated. That indicated either a clotting problem or that not enough blood had been in the tube. An objective reaction would be to assume there was not enough blood in the tube and recheck it. My anxious reaction was to skip the reasoning and conclude I had end-stage liver disease. I paged Larry, and when he responded, I dissolved in tears.

"Roz, you shouldn't be checking your own blood tests!" Larry chided. "It's a lab error! We'll have to get it rechecked. I'm sure it's fine."

"You're always sure everything's fine," I accused. "It's not fine. I'm sure they drew enough blood. I don't think it's a mistake."

"There's nothing I can say that's going to convince you. Just get the blood rechecked." He hung up abruptly, obviously peeved at my neurotic fears.

I went back to the lab and had them redraw my blood. I wrote "STAT" on the slip. A few hours later, I found the results on my desk. Normal. I felt stupid. But mostly I felt relieved.

But what about the bruises? I found one of the nurses in the office, an older woman who'd been doing patient care for 25 years, and asked her to go over the technique for injecting oneself subcutaneously. Apparently, I'd been doing it wrong. The needle was supposed to be inserted at a 90-degree angle to my thigh. There were no more bruises once I changed my technique.

THOUGH OUR MOVE to the suburbs was planned and we were happy to be leaving the city, the move was more chaotic than we had hoped. We were in the midst of a buyer's market in Philadelphia and felt lucky to have sold our home at all. While our house in the suburbs would not be vacated until January, our buyer wanted the row home November 1, so we had to move to an apartment for the interim. We found a large furnished one in our city neighborhood, and the landlord was willing to put up with our dog. So in late fall of 1991, we began to prepare for our move.

My routine existence—commuting to work, practicing medicine as a fairly new doctor, caring for a baby—was hardly stress-free, but I knew my way around it well. Somehow, I took and passed my internal medicine boards, so another task could be checked off. After surviving residency and boards, a move had, from a distance, looked like a piece of cake. Yet social scientists tell us that a change of address rates up among the top ten stressors and is associated with stress-related illness. I was already feeling depleted, and our move seemed overwhelming when it actually arrived. Not only did we have to move, we had to do it twice. We would pack our things, put them in storage for two months, and move into the furnished apartment, and we would do this knowing that another move was imminent.

I started to pack some boxes of holiday dishes and other things we didn't need on a day-to-day basis a month ahead of time. The energy required to wrap, carry, and pack was all the strength I had. After a few days of packing after work in the evenings, I was so exhausted that I could barely stand. My stomach started to hurt more than usual, and I started having migraines every afternoon. Larry told me to stop packing.

"I'll do it. You can't. It's going to wear you out," he said.

"How can you pack our whole household alone?" I exclaimed. "That's too much work!"

"I'll get it done. Don't worry about it."

And he did. I sat, feeling helpless and guilty each night after Max went to sleep, and watched my husband single-handedly prepare us to move. He packed our dispensable items in boxes for the storage company to pick up and drove carloads of our necessities over to the new apartment.

We moved into the strange new building, and I thought the stress level would decrease. Instead, I felt worse. I hated the rickety elevator and the chemical smell in the hallway of the apartment building. I hated taking the laundry to the basement laundry room and inserting quarters in the slots. I hated the fire alarms that went off at odd hours, triggered by dust from construction in one wing of the building. I hated the teal and pink and chrome furniture that sparsely scattered our apartment. I hated my upstairs neighbor who complained that our dog's barking disturbed her. Most of all, I hated that we were going to have to move again very soon.

I came home from work early one January day, exhausted after an interferon injection the night before. I was going to pick up Max at family daycare on the way home, but I decided to leave him for another hour and take a nap. My head was aching, and it felt like a migraine was starting. I took my migraine medication and tried to lie down, but the pain got more and more intense, and I began to feel nauseated. I called Larry. He was in the midst of a meeting at the hospital and couldn't leave, but he said he'd pick up Max when he could. The medication still wasn't working, and I ran to the bathroom to vomit. The pill came up. The headache got worse, and I could barely move my head. I called my internist. He wasn't there, but his partner called me back. I explained about the interferon, the migraine, and the vomited medication.

"Go to the emergency room," he told me. "Get someone to drive you. This might just be a bad migraine, but you're on an experimental drug. Something else could be going on."

I felt way too sick to argue. I dialed my friend Debbie, who'd been a resident with me. I wanted a medical friend to go with me. No answer. I dialed my friend Jane, the one with the breast cancer. She was healthy again at this point, and her experience as a patient made her good moral support. She answered on the second ring.

"I have to ask you a big favor. I need a ride to the ER. I have a headache and I'm puking my guts out."

She was there almost immediately. I stumbled blindly out of the apartment into her car. The trip to the ER seemed to take years. We stopped frequently so I could open the door and throw up.

We arrived in the emergency room and I signed in. It was packed. We sat in the waiting room for almost an hour before I finally couldn't stand it, and I begged the charge nurse to put me in a dark room. A few minutes later, an intern came in. He looked five years old. He had no idea what interferon was. He couldn't see my retina when he looked in my eyes. He asked me what worked for my headaches. I told him I would need Demerol for this one. I vomited while I waited for the nurse to get the medication.

Miraculously, my own internist showed up while I was waiting. I was relieved beyond description. He looked in my eyes and did a neurological exam. He told me he thought the interferon had precipitated a particularly severe migraine. He told me I needed to decrease my stress if I was going to make it through the rest of the course.

It made sense in theory, but I couldn't figure out how to do it. Which of my tasks each day could I give up? I already felt I spent too little time with Max. I didn't have housework to do, since the apartment building supplied maid service once a week. The upcoming move was unavoidable, and anyway, Larry would pack the little bit of stuff in the apartment. Work? My career, the calling I had trained and sweated for? I couldn't stop working! What would my colleagues think of me? Nobody would take me seriously if I stopped working, even temporarily! How would I define myself if I quit working? No, that wasn't going to happen.

In the end, there was nothing I was willing to let go of. Larry tried to pick up the slack by doing the grocery shopping and other errands on the weekends, but the schedule remained largely the same, and I had lots of headaches but managed to stay out of the ER.

We moved into our new house in March. After the first days of unpacking and getting adjusted, much of the emotional stress lifted. I was also in the home stretch with the interferon—just a few more weeks to go. All the monthly blood tests were normal. I had high hopes. I began to believe the nightmare would end.

The evening of my last injections was an auspicious occasion. I ceremoniously deposited the last syringe and needle into my sharps container, then put the container in my car so that I could dispose of it at the hospital the next day. I was free.

CHAPTER 10

# Losing Hope

I RELAPSED. IT TOOK only two weeks. My liver enzymes went from normal, as they'd been since the first week of interferon, to three times normal, as they'd been before treatment. I felt better physically than I had during treatment, but no better than I had before treatment. It was as if the biopsy and the months of interferon had never happened, had been a bad dream, only now things were worse, because now there was no hope of eradicating this virus. Of course, I'd known this was likely. No promises had been made. Interferon was experimental. The odds had been against me. None of that lessened the disappointment.

I sat on a plastic chair in the little exam room back in Dr. Paynes's office, with the lights glaring. The nurse told me to put on an exam gown, but I refused. There was nothing for him to examine. I was only there to talk, and I didn't want to do that, either. I was not anxious or hopeful or angry, as I'd been at other visits with him. I felt nothing. I read my medical journals (this time I brought work, knowing I'd be waiting a good while for him).

He walked in, only 30 minutes behind schedule, in his usual flurry of scattered papers and wrinkled clothing. He looked at me quizzically, having expected to find me sitting on the exam table in a gown.

"I'm sure you saw the labs," I said.

"Yes, I know you've relapsed. But you were a short-term responder. The protocol allows one attempt at re-treatment for responders. You could start again in August, after a three-month break."

"If the interferon didn't work this time, why would we think it would work if we did it again?" I asked.

"Well, we really have no reason to think it would, but we don't know. It's possible that it would."

"It doesn't make sense to me. I don't think I want to get more treatment right now." I hadn't expected him to offer me more treatment, but considering it then, I had no desire to go through the same miserable regimen again, only to be back in the same place a few months down the road.

"I can understand wanting to take some time off from treatment," Dr. Payne said. "You don't have to start that soon if you don't want to. You could wait until later in the fall if you want."

"No, I mean I don't think I want this treatment again at all. I think I need to wait until there's something else. Besides, I'm thinking about getting pregnant. My health probably isn't going to get better in the near future, so it seems like if I'm going to have another baby I should do it soon. I've been reading. There doesn't seem to be any contraindication to pregnancy. What do you think?"

"I think you should get treated again before thinking about pregnancy."

"Why? It doesn't sound like a year or two is going to make a difference to my course. Why do I need to get treated now?" I knew I was challenging his authority, but I needed to know.

"You're right, a year or two doesn't matter. But you wouldn't be eligible for the study anymore if you wait that long. Besides, I don't get why you want another kid so badly. I have two, and I don't think it's so great."

At first, I wondered whether I'd misheard him. Then I wanted to scream. I stared at him instead. At that moment, my relationship with Dr. Payne was severed.

"I think I'll take my chances," I told him, trying not to let him see my hands trembling. I picked up my things and left, knowing I'd never go back.

Before I was diagnosed with hep C, I never thought much about choosing a doctor. Strange as it may seem for a physician to say this, I really didn't care much who I went to for care as long as the person was knowledgeable and came with a recommendation from someone I trusted. My parents picked my pediatrician, family doctor, and ophthalmologist when I was young. When I had the rheumatoid nodules as a teenager, my parents chose a hand surgeon and a rheumatologist. Gynecologic care came at college and medical school without a choice; we all went to the nurse-practitioner at the student health center. When I needed a gastroenterologist, that nurse-practitioner referred me to one of the senior physicians at the medical school. It never occurred to me to look elsewhere. When I got pregnant with Max, I asked my medical friends who had delivered their babies. I never felt strongly connected to any of these doctors, but I wasn't really looking for a connection. They were good enough for the circumstances.

Everything changed with the hepatitis. This time it mattered to me whether I felt comfortable, cared for, and understood. I began to understand the importance of the chemistry between doctor and patient.

Once some time passed, I stopped believing that Dr. Payne was a monster. Inarguably, he was not particularly sensitive or tactful, but he was not malicious or incompetent. My feeling that he had failed me, and my intensely negative feelings toward him, came out of the fact that he was very limited in the social/emotional realm and we were horribly mismatched.

I, too, have failed patients. I'm introspective and willing to take emotional risks, so I think it happens fairly infrequently; I try to tune in to my patients' needs. But sometimes I miss the boat, or I simply can't meet their needs. I have to forgive myself when this happens. In the same vein, I had to forgive Dr. Payne. I think he did the best he could with me. He didn't have a clue what I needed, so giving it to me wasn't even an option.

So, in time, I forgave him. But I learned an essential lesson. I would carefully select my next hepatologist. I lived in a major East Coast city with seven academic medical centers. There had to be an appropriate doctor for me.

I looked through the medical school faculty lists and asked friends at each institution what they thought of their GI and hepatology faculty. As it turned out, there were only a handful of specialists treating hepatitis C in the area. One was a former professor, and I knew we would not do well together. Another worked with Dr. Payne, so he was out. A third was affiliated with a non-teaching hospital, so was unlikely to be involved in cutting-edge research. Finally, I settled on meeting with Dr. Hope at one of the major medical schools in the city. I had met him years earlier when he was a GI fellow at the hospital where I was doing some rotations as a student. He had seemed bright and was very personable.

I made an appointment to meet with Dr. Hope. I gathered all my records and test results, and picked up my biopsy slides from the pathology department at the Hospital of the University of Pennsylvania. I wanted to arrive prepared. I wanted Dr. Hope to have all the information he would need to give me good advice. But more than that, I wanted Dr. Hope to like me, to see me as a "good patient." I wasn't looking for more treatment right at the moment, but I knew I needed a doctor to follow my progress, and to prescribe treatment when I was ready.

I went to the appointment alone. I wasn't scared; the things I feared had already happened. I waited in a tastefully understated waiting room, all dark wood and neutral upholstery, with a dozen or so other patients and their companions. The nurse called my name after about 20 minutes and escorted me to an exam room. The room was like every other exam room I'd ever been in—harsh fluorescent lights and beige tile flooring, an uncomfortable straight chair, a desk, and a blue exam table. There was nothing new about the surroundings. The nurse took my blood pressure and temperature. She didn't tell me to get undressed, which was a good sign, in my opinion. She left the room.

Dr. Hope came in minutes later. He greeted me and looked at my chart, labeled with "M.D." after my name.

"You look familiar," he said. "Have we crossed paths in the hospital?"

"A long time ago—I was a medical student and you were a fellow. My last name was Barsky then—I use my married name now."

"Are you practicing medicine?" he asked.

"Yes, I'm a general internist in Bryn Mawr," I answered.

"Well, you're obviously not here to talk about the practice of medicine. I reviewed the records you faxed. So I know about the hepatitis C and your relapse off interferon. How can I help you now?"

"I'm not entirely sure," I admitted. "I need to change hepatologists. Dr. Payne and I just didn't mesh. I'm thinking about trying to have a second child. I don't think I want to go through the interferon thing again unless there are some major improvements in the protocol and the odds. I just need some advice."

"Well, you're not sick from the hepatitis now. I looked at your slides, too. There's inflammation, but it's pretty mild. I think you can put off treatment for a couple years. There's not any clear contraindication to pregnancy. Just as long as you realize that there is a small risk that the infection could be passed to the baby."

I felt as though I'd been on a long, arduous journey and had finally returned home. This man was making sense to me. I was in my comfort zone, and we could talk to each other.

"Is there anything new in terms of treatment?" I asked.

"Well, not yet, but there will probably be an improved protocol ready to go by next fall," he told me.

"So would you be willing to monitor things with me for now?"

"I wish I could, but I'm not going to be here. I just accepted a position in Boston, and I'll be leaving Philly in July. I'm also not sure who's going to pick up my patients yet. I'd have to refer you to a colleague."

"I can't believe it," I said. "I'm not sure there's anybody else here I'd want to go to."

"There are some other people in the GI division here who are good, and they're getting up to speed on hep C. Let me give you names."

I took the names but knew I wouldn't call. I couldn't deal with any more disappointments.

# CHAPTER 11

# Life Belongs to the Living

I SAT ON THE closed seat of the toilet in my black-and-yellow tiled bathroom, staring at the little white plastic square in front of me. A pale-blue line appeared, then a second one. Two blue lines—positive test. Just as I thought, I was pregnant. I couldn't help smiling. Larry would be home from work soon. I left the plastic square on the sink where he'd be sure to see it.

Larry and I had lots of challenges in our lives, but infertility wasn't one of them. We'd barely stopped using contraception after weeks of deliberation about whether this was the right time. I'd had to wait until I'd been off interferon for three months before we could even consider it. In the meantime, I'd started a new job, in a clinic run by one of the teaching hospitals, as the commute to my previous job had been very difficult. Getting pregnant at the start of a brand-new job was not ideal, but there never was a "good" time, and I felt under a certain amount of pressure to complete my childbearing while my health was satisfactory. It was hard to predict what might happen with the hep C.

Anyway, I was thrilled, though a little apprehensive, that it had happened so fast. I wanted to enjoy the idea of a new baby before I faced the realities of getting OB care, informing my employer, and preparing Max for a sibling.

Once the whole thing sunk in, I decided I'd need to seek out an obstetrician earlier rather than later. The OB I'd used for my first pregnancy had been nice enough, but I'd mentioned the hep C to him at my annual visit and he seemed to know very little about it. In addition, the circumstances of Max's birth had made for a bad experience. I wanted to start fresh, and with someone who knew medicine as well as obstetrics. I called one of the female OBs I'd met in some phase of my training, who had a reputation for being quick and knowledgeable. She had delivered babies to other patients with hep C, she told me, and was reasonably up-to-date on the topic. She'd be happy to take me on as a patient.

I had my first visit with Dr. Sharp, who urged me to call her Deb, and I immediately felt comfortable. She asked me whether I had any additional worries about the pregnancy.

"I'd really prefer not to have another cesarean section, if it can be avoided," I told her.

"Well, you know I can't promise, but we can make every effort to do a VBAC [vaginal birth after cesarean]. We'll have to see how big the baby is towards delivery, and see how you and the baby both are then. If everything seems fine, we'll try it."

I was relieved to hear this, and even felt at ease enough to bring up my postpartum depression.

"Don't worry," she said, "we'll just stay very aware of the possibility that it could happen again, and if it does, treat it aggressively. But it's much more common with first babies, and you had bad circumstances. It may not recur at all."

I wasn't ready yet to discuss my concerns regarding passing hep C to the baby. We'd get to that, in time.

I was totally satisfied with my visit; I felt as though the bases were covered, and Deb would do everything she could to make this birth a better experience. I knew I could talk to her, and I trusted her judgment.

I hoped my own patients left their visits with me feeling the same way. In my new clinic job, I faced a significant challenge. I was scheduled to see four patients every hour. At this point, every patient was new to me, and 15 minutes was not enough time to learn much about a patient with complicated problems. If someone came in for a sore throat or a routine blood pressure check, it was fine. I could spend the first few minutes putting the patient at ease and getting a history. The rest of the time would then be spent examining what needed to be examined, explaining my impression and plan to the patient, and writing any necessary prescriptions and instructions. But if there were several problems to address, and especially if any of those problems had emotional significance, I needed more time.

Many of the visits to the clinic were, as is common in medical practice, for symptoms of depression or anxiety. These patients needed more than a prescription; they needed reassurance and support. Though they usually would have benefited from psychotherapy, there were numerous barriers—from cultural prohibitions to lack of resources—that meant most would never get it. I was it—the provider of medication, practical suggestions, understanding, and support. A hard role to play in 15-minute increments.

A patient didn't need to have a psychiatric diagnosis for his or her needs to be complex.

Once, a young woman from an African country came in for a routine checkup. She had no known medical problems and voiced no complaints. I suggested the usual tests for this situation: a urinalysis, a cholesterol check, and a Pap smear. When I brought up the Pap smear, she became extremely agitated. She was well educated and told me she knew how important the test was, but that she could not allow me to do it. My first thought was that she'd been sexually abused, and I questioned her appropriately. No, she told me, she hadn't been abused. Well, not exactly. You see, in her country…

It suddenly became clear. I remembered the documentary I'd seen on female circumcision in certain African tribes. A girl as young as eight or nine was subjected to crude surgery on her labia, vagina, and clitoris that, in effect, prevented her from having sexual pleasure as a woman. I told her I'd heard about this. She was relieved that her secret was out. With patience and a lot of reassurance, we managed the Pap smear. Then there was the matter of talking through her feelings about the surgery and how it had affected her. No, 15 minutes was not going to be enough.

I learned to be efficient, to manipulate the schedule (five minutes for the uncomplicated sore throat and 25 for the victim of domestic violence), and to bring patients back for repeat visits if necessary. I managed to stay less than a half-hour behind on most days.

I think I usually inspired confidence in my patients. But I was pretty stressed by the pace. I didn't know that things were only going to get worse as managed care and other discount insurance plans crept into existence, putting more and more pressure on the medical system.

Fortunately, my life was more than the stress of my job. I worked part-time, and played Mommy to Max the rest of the time. He had changed from a colicky baby to an exuberant, lively, talkative toddler. Outings with him were a joy; we went to the library, the park, the museums, and the zoo. I was also greatly enjoying my pregnancy. Unlike during the first pregnancy, I was in maternity clothes by the tenth week. Rather than lament the loss of my figure, I was proud of my pregnant belly, and I was excited about the new baby. The pregnancy was easy and uncomplicated; I never even had morning sickness, and I felt good, if a little fatigued.

My busy life and the pregnancy kept me distracted, for the most part, from my concerns about my long-term health. Thoughts of hepatitis C would creep into my head, but an inner voice would say, "This is not the time to worry about that; you're otherwise occupied right now."

I had my monthly visits with Dr. Deb, and each time, all was okay. We began to talk about how hepatitis C would affect my childbirth and my baby.

"I've been reading about HIV, and I know it's not the same," I told her, "but some researchers think infection of the baby during birth is less likely if the baby is delivered by C-section."

"The risk of infection is extremely low for vaginal birth in the case of hep C," Deb said. "HIV would be more of a risk. I don't think you need to have a C-section because of this, if all is otherwise okay for a vaginal birth." One concern down, two to go.

"What about breastfeeding? I can't find much in the literature. Will I increase the baby's risk by breastfeeding?"

"Nobody seems to be sure. I talked to some Infectious Disease people, and the general consensus is that you should probably bottle-feed."

I was disappointed, but I'd prepared myself for this possibility. I could deal with this. A few years later, it was determined that, in fact, it is safe for mothers with hepatitis C to breastfeed, but I had to go on the knowledge we had at the time.

"Okay," I said. "Last question. What do you think about testing the baby?"

"You'll need to talk to your pediatrician about that one. I haven't a clue." I loved her honesty.

I called the pediatrician. I needed to talk to her anyway. I hadn't forgotten about Max's apnea, and there'd been a SIDS (sudden infant death syndrome) death in the family since then. Since Larry had had an infant brother who also died of SIDS, there was now a concern about some kind of familial tendency for infants to have abnormal breathing patterns. It seemed to me that the new baby should be put on an apnea monitor for safety reasons, and I needed to discuss this with the pediatrician.

"Well, you've got two tough questions," the pediatrician told me. "As far as getting the baby tested for hep C, you can't get an accurate test for the first eighteen months anyway."

At that time, the only test was an antibody test, which would come up positive for a period because the baby would get antibodies from me, which would take a while to disappear. A positive antibody test in that situation would not mean that the baby was infected. Now there are more accurate and sophisticated tests that can be performed on infants.

"After that, it would be up to you to decide," she continued. "There's no treatment approved for children anyway, so maybe you don't want to know. On the other hand, it's likely to prove the baby is not infected, and that would give you reassurance. Why don't you see how you feel at the time?

"As for the question of the apnea monitor, it sounds right to me. But I think you should contact the neonatologist at the hospital where you're going to deliver. They're the experts, and they're the ones who would set you up with the monitor anyway."

I called the neonatologist and set up a meeting. He listened to our family history and the saga of Max and his apnea. He was pleasant and matter-of-fact.

"You know we still have a very poor understanding of the relationship between apnea in newborns and SIDS. In theory, an apnea monitor will not prevent a SIDS death; if it's going to happen, it presumably will happen even if the parents are alerted to apnea and try to resuscitate the child. But with this kind of a family history, I think you're right. A test for apnea and an apnea monitor are advisable. I'll make sure it's set up for you as soon as the baby is born. By the way, SIDS is much less common in girls, so if it's a girl you can have a little more reassurance."

One more task accomplished. Now I could get back to a

normal existence until I got close to my due date, which was eight weeks away.

Five weeks later, I awoke on the morning of my routine OB check-up, took my shower, and got dressed. I looked in the mirror. I was wearing a white top and a huge black-and-white checked jumper. Something looked strange. I'd been carrying the baby "straight out in front" so that I looked like I had a basketball under my clothes. But today I looked flatter and wider. Maybe the baby had dropped into place for delivery? But then the baby kicked me. In the left side. Now, that was odd! I'd been getting kicked a lot, but more towards the front. I felt around. I could clearly feel feet at my left side, and head at my right side.

Ten minutes later I was in my OB's office. She examined me, and agreed; the baby was no longer head down, as it should have been and had been for weeks. An ultrasound confirmed it.

"How can that happen?" I asked in amazement. "I thought that once the pregnancy is this far along, the baby doesn't have enough room to turn itself."

"Well, that's usually the case. But you're defying the odds. The heartbeat is strong, though, and the baby is about six pounds already."

"So what does this mean? The baby is breech? Does that mean I'll need a C-section?"

"Technically the position is called transverse, back down," Deb told me. "Let me tell you the options. You can wait it out, and if the baby is still in this position the week before you're due, we'll do an elective C-section. I wouldn't try to deliver a transverse lay vaginally. Very honestly, transverses are unlikely to turn back to a head-down position. The other option, what I'd recommend if you want to avoid a cesarean, is to have a version."

"What does that mean?" I asked.

"You go to the hospital, and the high-risk obstetric doctors try to turn the baby by pushing on your belly in the right way. It's done under ultrasound. The sooner it's done, the more likely it will work, before the baby gets any bigger. The hitch is, the version often puts the mother into labor, so you might end up delivering right then and there. Which is okay, since you're far enough along for the baby to be born."

"Do you think it would work?" I was getting nervous. These complications reminded me of my complicated delivery with Max.

"You've got a good shot. Do you want me to set it up?"

"Let me call Larry. I think so, but I need his input."

"Okay, why don't you call me later. Just let me know before three so I can get things set up for tomorrow."

I left her office in a daze. This version thing sounded very unpleasant. And I wasn't ready to have this baby yet! But if I didn't do it, it sounded like a C-section was inevitable. I didn't want that either. I called Larry.

"Let's go for it," he said. "I've seen them done. It's not that bad. And if we have to be ready for the baby now, we'll be ready."

I tossed and turned all night. I called out from work in the morning, and got dressed in my favorite huge black maternity leggings and a comfortable top. No food before this procedure. I was ready to go. I waited for Larry to return from dropping Max at daycare. I felt sick.

We drove to Pennsylvania Hospital and found our way to the high-risk obstetrics suite. We sat in yet another bland beige waiting area. I went into the ladies' room. Suddenly, I felt a huge kick from the baby. Not just a normal kick, but almost like a big wave inside. I felt my belly. No feet on the left. No head on the right. I looked in the mirror. Straight out in front.

I went out into the waiting area. "Larry, the baby turned itself again," I blurted out.

"What do you mean?"

"I mean, its head is down again."

"Are you sure?"

"Pretty sure."

"Kaplan!" called the nurse. We were ushered into a large exam room with ultrasound equipment. Two doctors in scrubs were adjusting dials on the machine.

"Hi, I'm Dr. Dobbs and this is Dr. Johnson."

"Roz Kaplan. This is my husband, Larry. I'm not sure I need to be here anymore. I think the baby turned back."

"Well, why don't we do an ultrasound and find out?" Dr. Dobbs suggested.

I hopped up on the table. The nurse helped me adjust my top up and my waistband down, and put ultrasound gel on my belly. The doctor ran the ultrasound probe over me.

"You're absolutely right," he told me. "Your daughter is head-down again."

"Daughter?" Larry said.

"You didn't know the sex?"

"No, they couldn't tell when the routine ultrasound was done before," I said. I was ecstatic. Of course, I would have been happy with any healthy baby, but I secretly wanted a daughter desperately. And she was back in the right position. Someone was looking out for me. Maybe my luck was changing.

"Well, you can go home and wait until you go into labor," said Dr. Johnson. "I don't know why this happened, but it's not very likely to happen again. Good luck."

I had a few more weeks to go, according to the dates. The baby-flipping incident had unnerved me, and I was tired. I decided to stop working and go on maternity leave early. It was unlike me, but I didn't want to take any chances with my health or the baby's now.

My due date was April 5, a Sunday. It came and went without a single contraction. I saw my obstetrician the next day. I told her I was worried that the scenario with Max's birth would be repeated.

"There's no reason to think that. Everything's fine, and it's common to go post-dates. Come back next Monday if you haven't gone into labor by then. Don't worry!" Easy for her to say!

The week crept by. I was physically uncomfortable and getting increasingly worried, though the baby seemed active and kicked me all day long. Sunday was Easter, though it was a cold and crisp day that felt more like November. We decided to take Max to the zoo to get my mind off my overdue labor. The zoo was fun, but it didn't work. I felt as though I couldn't stand being pregnant one more minute.

After the zoo, we went to a neighbor's Easter egg hunt. Another neighbor, a midwife, was there. She watched me haul my body in the door.

"Haven't you had that baby yet?" Kate asked me.

"I wish! I feel like I'm going to go crazy if I don't have her soon. Can you wave your wand over me or something?"

"No, but you could take some castor oil. I've seen it work before."

"Really? I've heard of it, but I thought it was a myth. Is it safe?"

"Sure. The worst that can happen is you'll get diarrhea."

I was ready to do it. "How much do you take?" I asked.

"You mix two tablespoons with a glass of orange juice. Then put a teaspoon of baking soda in so it doesn't upset your stomach," she directed.

"Larry, will you take me to the drugstore to get castor oil?" I asked when we left the party.

"What are you talking about?" he asked.

I told him Kate's recipe. He shook his head.

"You are crazy! Are you really going to do that?"

"Yes! I can't stand this anymore! I'll do anything!"

"You really are nuts," he told me. "Okay, but we'll have to drive out to Wayne to the all-night pharmacy. Nothing's open on Easter."

A couple of hours later, I stood at the kitchen counter, measuring the castor oil into a glass. I reached into the refrigerator for orange juice. We were out. Oh well, I'd have to use cranberry juice. I wasn't about to send Larry out for orange juice at this point.

I mixed the juice and the oil. The oil rose right back to the top and lay there, a clear layer on the dark red liquid. Okay, now the baking soda.

Like a nightmare from my chemistry lab days, the red acidic

juice turned blue and foamed with the addition of the base. It bubbled like a witches' brew. I held my nose and gulped it down.

By 10 P.M., nothing had happened. Larry went to bed, anticipating a busy Monday at work. I couldn't relax. I went into the living room and turned on the TV. I flipped the channels. *The Graduate* was on one of the cable channels. I sat down to watch.

Simon and Garfunkle had just finished a rousing chorus of "Mrs. Robinson" when the first contraction hit. At first I wasn't sure, because it was a strong pain in my lower back rather than in my pelvis. But ten minutes later, another came, and then another after about the same interval. After a couple of hours, I was pretty sure it was labor.

I went upstairs and poked Larry, who was sound asleep.

"I think I'm in labor," I said.

Larry is very hard to awaken, and he didn't really hear me the first time. So I kind of hit him.

"What? What is it?" he half-yelled, half-mumbled.

"I said, I think I'm in labor. Or else I have a kidney infection. I'm having back pains every few minutes."

"You're just imagining it because you took that castor oil," Larry said.

"I don't think I'm imagining it."

"But you're not sure, right? So take a Tylenol and go to sleep. If it's really labor, you'll know soon."

Larry hates to get up when he's sleeping and will do just about anything to get out of it. Still, I wasn't positive, so I lay down. I was tired, and I figured I'd see how I felt. I couldn't get comfortable, though, and I had to pee every ten minutes, so I kept getting up. And the pains were still coming about ten minutes apart, maybe a little less. So I called the OB.

Deb wasn't on call. Instead, one of her partners, a man we knew socially as well as through Deb's practice, called back. I told him what I was feeling.

"You're definitely in labor," he said. "You're having back labor. You can wait until the contractions get a little closer, but then you'd better go over to the hospital."

I decided to let Larry have as much rest as possible. I lay down, planning to wait until the contractions were seven minutes apart. By four A.M., they were, and I shook Larry hard. This time, he didn't argue. He could see I was serious. He called our brother-in-law to come stay with Max. He arrived in minutes, and we headed out the door.

Fifteen hours later, after a long but uncomplicated labor, our new baby was emerging.

"That's a cute baby!" Deb exclaimed. I was between pushes and I wasn't interested in her opinion at that moment, since the baby's shoulders were stuck, and I was gasping to get enough air for the next push. With the next contraction, I pushed the shoulders out, along with the rest of my daughter. And while catching her, Deb got a blood splash in her right eye. I saw it happen. And I immediately thought, *Oh God, she's been exposed to my blood.* For that instant, time was suspended, and the exhilaration and joy of my newly born infant was not the focus. Deb handed the baby to the nurse. She calmly went to the sink and rinsed her eye.

And then Madeline Rose Kaplan was in my arms, and nothing else mattered.

I didn't forget the blood splash. When Deb came to see me the next day, I told her I was worried about it. She told me she wasn't. "Low-risk exposure," she reminded me. I made her promise to get tested in three months. (She did, and it was negative.) I was thankful for her presence of mind and professionalism.

Maddy Rose and I left the hospital in 36 hours with no complications. Maddy was, undeniably, an unusually pretty baby, with a perfectly round, bald head, delicate features, and ivory-and-pink skin. She went home on her apnea monitor for preventative reasons, but all looked well with her breathing tests and the monitor was silent. I had not the slightest dip in mood, not even a hint of "baby blues." It felt like a new beginning, as though some of the bad experiences of the last few years had been undone. It felt like the tide was turning.

The next year flew by. Maddy was an easy baby, as calm and quiet as Max had been raucous. She slept well and predictably, giving me time with Max when she was asleep. Nevertheless, it didn't take long for his sibling rivalry to be aroused, and Larry and I spent much time and energy trying to let him know he was still loved and appreciated.

I went back to work after eight weeks and fought the losing battle to keep the balance between work and mothering. It never really was balance, but rather was more like a seesaw ride, with first one end up and then the other. It wasn't bad, but it wasn't easy. I changed jobs yet again, when an opportunity arose to work in a private-practice situation with several women I liked and respected. As with all transitions, it was an adjustment. I was tired.

Fatigue brought me back to the old worries. My life was

moving along, and time was going by. I never forgot about the hep C, but I had avoided dealing with it directly for two full years. Now it was starting to prod at me. The cloud swirled closer to my head. Perhaps it was time to consider treatment again.

# CHAPTER 12

# Guinea Pig, Take Two

I N THE WORLD of inpatient medicine, we always say "don't get admitted to the hospital in July," for that is when all the new interns and residents start their rotations. True, it seems dangerous to have an intern on his or her first day in the hospital, with his or her shiny-new MD degree, writing medication orders for you or diagnosing your myocardial infarction. But July is not the only unsafe time on the hospital wards. The truth is, the hospital is always a dangerous place. Mistakes are made, problems go unnoticed, nurses are overworked, and doctors are overtired. The only reason to get admitted to a hospital is if your condition is more dangerous than being in there.

The hospital is dangerous no matter who you are and what you know.

Maddy was a year old when I had my second liver biopsy. It had taken a while, once I started to think seriously about more treatment, to find the right doctor. I had gotten to know

Dr. Lennie Middleman, a new liver specialist at Cooper Hospital in Camden, New Jersey, through my husband, who worked there.

Lennie was different from the hepatologists I'd met in the past. He was warm, enagaging, and encouraging. He told me that re-treatment with interferon might work better if length of treatment was determined by when the virus could no longer be detected in the blood. This theory was still under investigation, but it seemed worth a shot. The catch was that he wanted a new liver biopsy before I started, to see whether there had been any change with time or with the first course of interferon. I balked at this after my last experience, mostly because of the anxiety, but also because I had hated staying overnight in the hospital. Lennie assured me that he, unlike Dr. Payne, could give me sedation to make the procedure easier, and that he would do it under ultrasound in the GI lab rather than at the bedside, so that inadequate tissue would be unlikely. So I agreed and I reported to the gastroenterology procedure unit early one spring morning.

Larry took the morning off to stay with me, and we sat behind my little privacy curtain in the GI suite and chatted while we waited for Lennie. I wasn't really frightened this time. The nurse put in an IV for my sedation, and Lennie showed up on time. I watched the ultrasound image of my liver as the sedative went in through the IV. It seemed like a second later when I awoke and the biopsy was over. At first I was fine, until I tried to take a breath and a horrible searing pain went through my right side. I remember saying "I can't breathe," and Lennie saying "Give her more Versed, she's panicking," and then I was out again.

When I awoke a few minutes later, however, the pain was

still there. I realized I could breathe, but it was excruciatingly painful. I told this to Lennie and Larry. Lennie wasn't sure what was wrong. The possibilities included pneumothorax (a collapsed lung from a poorly directed biopsy needle), bleeding into my liver capsule, and hysteria. I think everyone else thought it was the last, but I knew it wasn't. I was sent for a chest X-ray, which revealed no pneumothorax, and blood samples were ordered every two hours to make sure I wasn't losing excessive blood into my liver capsule. Still in tremendous pain, I was taken to a hospital room at the end of a long hallway on one of the general medical floors. Lennie came in to say that my first blood test showed only minor bleeding and that he had to leave to go to Baltimore. He was leaving me under the watchful eye of his fellow, a nice but inexperienced young woman. He didn't want to give me any pain medication until after the next blood test, so as not to mask a serious problem. The fellow would follow up on this. Larry sat with me for a couple of hours, feeling helpless, because I was in too much pain to converse.

Interestingly, I knew I was not dying. I just wanted pain relief, and it was not forthcoming. Like the first time I was biopsied, I was not allowed to move for several hours, but I had no inclination to do so, since movement exacerbated the pain. After a while, I told Larry to leave—it was easier to manage the discomfort alone, since I couldn't be distracted from the acute pain. I just had to sink into it, and I did. Time was suspended within this pain. Maybe I lay there for an hour, or maybe it was five hours. It grew dark outside my window. No nurse came to look in on me. I wondered whether my blood test was back; maybe I could get some pain medication. I pushed the call button.

"Yes?" came a staticky voice.

"I need a nurse," I said.

"What do you need from a nurse?" asked the voice.

"I have a question, and I need something for pain."

"Do you have an order for pain medicine?"

"That's the question." It was taking all my energy to talk through the knife sticking in my side.

"Someone will be there soon," the voice said.

I waited for what seemed like a century. I realized I had to go to the bathroom. Was I allowed to get up? It had been hours. Maybe I would try. But even the slightest movement caused a lancing feeling that took my breath away. I decided I would have to wait for the nurse and get a bedpan. I waited another century. Then I rang the call bell again.

"Yes?" a different voice answered this time.

"I've been waiting for a nurse to ask about pain medicine. And now I have to go to the bathroom and I can't get up."

"Well, they're busy. I'll let your nurse know."

Time continued to crawl by. No one came. I rang the call bell again when the need to urinate was becoming unbearable.

"Yes?"

"I really need my nurse! This can't wait any longer!"

"Someone will be there as soon as they can," said the irritated voice.

I don't know how much time went by then, but it was at least another 15 minutes. Nobody came. I didn't even hear steps in the hall. I needed to get to the phone. It was on the nightstand next to the bed, but I would have to move over six inches and prop myself up to reach it. I wiggled over a couple of inches.

The knifelike pain stabbed me in the right chest. I waited until it calmed a bit, then inched over more. I pulled myself up by the bed rail. Again, I felt I was being stabbed, but I clutched the phone and pulled it into the bed with me. I caught my breath. Whom should I call? Larry was the obvious person, but I had no idea where he was, because I had no idea what time it was. I guessed by the length of time it had been dark that it must be after 7:00, and he would be at home with the kids. I dialed my home number. He answered on the third ring.

"You have to help me!" I said. "They've left me here. I still can't breathe. It still hurts just as much. I have to pee, and I can't get to the bathroom! I've called over and over for the nurse, and nobody came."

Larry said he'd call the nurses' station right away. He must have given them an earful, because moments later, a burly male nurse was there to help me. He seemed completely shocked that I could not just get out of bed on my own. No one from the previous shift had signed out that I was in pain. He paged the fellow, who arrived a few minutes later. She said my blood test showed a slight drop in the blood count, indicating I'd bled into my liver capsule, which accounted for the pain. She agreed to some pain medication, and the nurse returned with some Demerol after she'd left.

"What did she order?" I asked.

"Demerol, twenty-five milligrams," he said.

"Twenty-five milligrams wouldn't help a bee sting!" I said.

"Well, that's all she ordered. Why don't we wait and see if you feel better after it?"

Being a "drug-seeking" patient is a sure way to stop doctors and nurses from wanting to help you, so I shut up. I took the injection and waited, hoping it would at least take the edge off the pain. When it didn't, I called the nurse, who paged the fellow and asked for a larger dose. He came back to me saying, "She won't give you more—she doesn't want to mask pain." At this point, it seemed pointless to have all this pain. It wasn't telling us anything, it was just pain. But it was clear I was not getting anything else.

I lay awake for a very long time after that, afraid to move because it hurt so much and unable to sleep for the same reason. I started to need the bathroom again and debated ringing for the nurse, but I didn't want to deal with the staticky voice and its irritation again. Then, for no apparent reason, the pain started to dissipate. I tried moving around. It didn't hurt that much anymore. I tried sitting up. It felt okay. I took a deep breath. That felt okay also. Finally, I got up out of bed and went to the bathroom. I was okay! I looked at my watch lying on the bathroom counter. It was 4 A.M. I got back in bed and slept until the fellow came to see me at 8:00. She was surprised to see me looking so much better. She wanted me to stay and have one more blood count checked.

"Absolutely not. I'm going home. If I feel this much better, I'm sure the blood count is not continuing to drop."

She reluctantly signed my discharge. I felt I was being released from hell.

Not only am I a physician, but I was also the wife of a senior staff physician at the hospital where all this took place. I dreaded to think what a layperson, with nobody to advocate for him or her, would have done in this situation, and what might have happened if something more serious than minor bleeding had occurred. I tried to be positive about the experience. After all, bad experiences are supposed to teach us something. So what did I learn from that hospital admission? To tell my patients to advocate for themselves, and ideally to also have someone else there to advocate for them.

I have to be fair here. While this type of neglect does sometimes occur in hospitals, it is not what I commonly see. I don't know why it happened the night after my liver biopsy. I suspect there was a staffing problem or an emergency that caused my needs to slip through the cracks. In the hospital where I admit my patients, the nurses are extremely well trained and attentive to the patients, and I rarely hear horror stories. But I still tell my patients that they must advocate for themselves, or have their family members do so, when any issues arise.

I hoped that I had also learned, through all the adversity of the previous few years, to be patient. But waiting for the results of my second biopsy was excruciating. Had I waited too long, allowing my liver to be seriously damaged by hepatitis C? Or was it possible that somehow, my liver had healed, and I would not even need treatment? No, I could discard that possibility, since my liver function tests were still significantly abnormal. The best I could hope for was stability. No change would mean that progression was slow. Then I could consider getting treatment now, or I could even put it off a bit longer. But why would I do that? That would be taking too much of a chance. I shouldn't tempt fate. Only it's possible that in the next couple of years, they'd come up with better treatment....

What was I doing? It was a complete waste of time and

energy to go through these mental gymnastics, since I had no idea what the biopsy showed.

Fortunately, I didn't have to wait too long. Lennie called me with the results just six days after the biopsy was done.

"You have inflammation and a little bit of bridging necrosis (medicalese for clumps of dying cells), but no scarring or cirrhosis," Lennie informed me.

"Has there been progression from the last biopsy?" I asked. I had provided him with the slides from Dr. Payne's biopsy.

"Not a lot," Lennie hedged.

"Not a lot, but some, is what you're telling me?" I wasn't going to let him soothe me.

"Yes, some. You should get treated."

"Well, thanks for being honest." I was going to cry, but not while I was on the phone with Lennie. "What's the next step?"

"Come in next week, and we'll get pre-treatment labs and go over the protocol," Lennie said.

I didn't want to be tired and sick again, but I looked forward to starting treatment for the psychological relief it would bring. I could have hope, believe that the toxic injections were working. I would be doing something about the problem. I hated problems that had no solutions. Treatment was a solution, at least for the time being.

At least this time I knew what the side effects would be, and I knew how to administer the injections. My current job was less taxing than the one I'd had the first time I was treated, and we were planning no moves or other major changes in our lives. In theory, it should be easier than the first time around.

I met with Lennie and got my prescriptions, instructions,

and the ever-present red "sharps disposal" container. I started my Sunday, Tuesday, and Thursday injection schedule. It was uneventful. I had the expected side effects of fatigue and malaise, but not much else happened. Just as with the first course, my liver function tests normalized within a month.

At three months, I had a viral titer done, to see whether I had cleared the virus from my bloodstream. Preliminary data said that early clearing of viremia was a good prognostic sign. But hepatitis C virus was still detected in my blood. Lennie said this was not a reason to stop treatment and did not necessarily mean I would not have a long-term remission. Despite my initial disappointment, I forged ahead.

After four months, I was very fatigued, and I knew I looked haggard. I had lost about ten pounds, which I did not believe to be obvious to others, but my clothes were loose.

At that time, I had begun medical consulting at a residential center that treated eating disorders. I had not sought out this niche; a close friend, a psychologist who worked at the facility, asked me if I'd be interested in the consultation job. It sounded very intriguing, but I told her I knew nothing about the medical complications of anorexia and bulimia. She said, "You'll learn it." So I talked the other women I was working with into sharing the responsibility with me, and we gave it a try. It turned out to be medically fascinating and psychologically challenging, and soon I was seeing many eating disorder patients in my office as well as at the residential center.

I had one patient, a brilliant and beautiful woman tortured by anorexia, whom I saw quite frequently to monitor her weight and general physical condition. At first, Marie was terrified of me and of her medical visits, but as time went on, we developed a relationship in which she learned she could trust and depend on me. As often happens during the more acute phases of an eating disorder, she came to depend heavily on my support when she had to gain weight and became anxious.

Marie was extremely observant and never missed a change in the office environment or my demeanor. Being eating disordered, she was especially aware of other women's bodies. The weight loss that seemed so insignificant to me took on tremendous meaning in Marie's mind, but she hesitated to bring it up. Since it was not my habit to talk about myself, and certainly not about my illness, it did not occur to me to bring it up. So it remained in the background of our relationship until she could no longer contain her anxiety.

One evening, after a visit with Marie, I answered a page. The answering service told me that Marie had left a message, saying she needed to speak with me as soon as possible. I called back, and she answered immediately.

"I know it's not my business, but I have to ask you something," she blurted out, talking a mile a minute. "What's wrong with you? Do you have cancer?"

I was astounded, but I took a deep breath and went into doctor mode. "Why would you be concerned about that?" I asked.

"You look sick. You've lost weight. You're pale. I've never seen you look like that before. I know something's wrong. Please tell me."

A thousand thoughts passed through my head in seconds. I could deny that there was a problem. Not a good idea, since Marie's perceptions were correct and needed to be validated. I could lie and say I had something minor, but I'm not a good liar. I could hedge and just say it's not cancer, but not tell her more. Yet that would leave her anxious. If I told the truth, what would happen? Would I feel intruded upon? Would she be repulsed, afraid of getting the disease from me? Would she worry too much? Maybe, but this was a chance I would have to take.

"Marie, do you know anything about hepatitis C?" I asked her.

"Yeah, I've read about it. I think one of my cousins has it. That's the one that's chronic, right?"

"Yes, and that's what I have. Not cancer. And it's not even the hepatitis that's making me sick. I decided to get treatment to see if I can get rid of the hepatitis, and that's making me lose weight and feel kind of tired. But it's only for a few months, and I'm not that sick from it."

"I'm so relieved!" she told me. "I was sure you had something awful and you were going to die! I mean, I'm sorry you have this, but it's not as bad as what I thought."

I breathed a sigh of relief. I felt kind of good having her know. Sometimes the secret started to wear at me. I knew there were some very conservative docs who would have said I had crossed boundaries, and had let the patient cross boundaries. But I knew in my heart it was the right thing.

After five months of interferon, my viral titers were negative. Lennie told me there was nothing to do but to stop the regimen after six months and hope for the best. He couldn't predict whether the remission would last. I was happy to stop, but I wasn't all that hopeful. Yet I told everyone else that I was. I knew I was lying, but I couldn't stand them feeling sorry for me. I let my friends, my colleagues, my in-laws, even my own family, believe that the whole thing was over with. Only Larry knew how pessimistic I felt.

My liver function tests were abnormal again a month after I stopped treatment. At least I expected it, I told myself. There was nothing else to do. No new regimens, no new ideas. And Lennie was moving to Maryland. I wondered whether there was a way to strengthen denial, the way you strengthen your muscles by lifting weights. Mine was weak, and I needed it to work harder.

# CHAPTER 13

# One More Chance

THERE HAS NEVER been anything as startlingly beautiful and hopeful, and at the same time as utterly tragic and frightening, for me as watching my children grow. I watched them move out of their babyhoods, a metamorphosis from chubby, gurgling beings into sturdy, tiny people with ideas of their own. Max established himself early as a fighter, brilliant and tough, perseverant and angry. He held on to each idea he had as though it were a precious diamond, and if it needed to be pried from him, his temper flared like a torch. Maddy was a lover, a sunny-side-up, sweet, pliable doll, aching to please. I watched it all with the mixture of wonder and worry that only a mother understands. Would Maddy learn to hold her ground when she needed to? Would Max realize that he would have to be flexible to survive in the world? Would I be there to help them figure it out?

We took them to the zoo and the natural history museum, to swimming lessons and concerts. We wanted them to know how to ski and play tennis and ice-skate, how to appreciate nature and music and art. We wanted them to be happy, and we knew that ultimately, happiness would be their own responsibility. And while we were raising our children and living our lives, hepatitis C was living with us, in the corners and under the beds.

I have a friend, another doctor, who also had hepatitis C, probably from a transfusion he got as a child. When he was offered treatment, he declined for several years, then tried it and discontinued it after a month because he felt tired. About a year ago, his first child was born. I ran into him recently and he told me he had started treatment and was going to finish it, even though it "whipped his butt." When I asked why he'd changed his mind, he said it was because he didn't want to end up with end-stage liver disease ten years from now and realize he'd cut short his time with his child. Similarly, I have always felt that I have to be here as long as I possibly can, to be with my kids.

As my children grew, I felt the time passing and wondered what that meant for my health. And I looked at Maddy now and then, realizing I still had not had her tested, and wondered whether I was making a mistake. The pediatrician said, "There's nothing you can do about it if she has it, so why bother finding out? If the test is positive, it will just upset you." Yes, and if it was negative, I could rest easier. But I couldn't bring myself to do it, at least not yet.

We didn't speak of hepatitis C. It was something we just had to live with, so it got swept into the corners of our lives. It crept into my consciousness many times every day, but I pushed away the thoughts. I don't think Larry thought about it much at all. It didn't seem to change the flow of daily activity, so we didn't discuss it. The kids didn't know anything about it, though I later learned from Max that he'd had a vague awareness of something being wrong with Mom but that it wasn't something to bring up. It wasn't discussed, but I feared that I would become ill, even need a liver transplant, and that the carefree childhood I wanted for my children would be diminished by the weight of my illness.

I was tired a lot. But wasn't this normal, given my busy life? Hard to say. I thought I had less energy than the average person my age, but energy levels are variable from person to person. Sometimes I had body aches and I often had headaches, but these symptoms were nonspecific. The only clear symptom of hepatitis C was my deep longing not to have it anymore.

I kept abreast of the literature. My *New England Journal of Medicine* and *Annals of Internal Medicine* came regularly, and I scanned the table of contents of each issue for any information relevant to hepatitis C. I grilled my colleagues who practiced gastroenterology for information on breakthroughs in treatment of hepatitis. I nagged at Larry to ask the GI specialists he worked with, also. But until 1997, more than five years after my second relapse after interferon, nothing was new.

In 1997, I began reading preliminary reports on the combination of interferon and ribavirin, an antiviral drug used for children with respiratory synctial virus. RSV can be a fatal respiratory illness in some children, and an aerosol form of ribavirin was used to treat it in the hospital. Now scientists were looking at the combination of interferon and an oral form of ribavirin for chronic hepatitis, hypothesizing that a combination of two drugs would be more likely to eradicate any resistant virus than a single drug. The very early reports looked good, so I set out to learn more.

I called the people I knew in gastroenterology and hepatology and was led back to the University of Pennsylvania, where a large trial of interferon plus ribavirin was starting. I was told that Dr. Payne and his colleagues had left the institution several years earlier but that there were some new hepatologists. Among them was Dr. Lerner, the principal investigator for the interferon/ribavirin trials.

Anxious to find out whether I was a candidate for combination treatment, I made an appointment with Dr. Lerner. It was set for six weeks from the day I called, and six weeks seemed like forever.

Finally, the day of my appointment arrived. I showed up at the suburban satellite office of the university GI practice and filled out forms. I was ushered to the nurses' station, where they checked my weight and vital signs and compiled a list of my medications. Then I sat in an exam room for what seemed an eternity. Finally, Dr. Lerner entered, a young-looking man with curly black hair and a kind face.

"I'm really sorry for keeping you waiting," he said. "They scheduled a new patient into a follow-up slot accidentally, and I got behind."

I understood this dilemma perfectly; it happened to me in my practice all the time. More importantly, he'd apologized for the tardiness.

He looked at the chart, with its pile of medical forms. "So you have hep C? How long has it been since you were last treated?"

"A good four years, maybe a little longer," I told him. "I was treated twice and relapsed both times. I'm hoping for something different."

"Well, we have the interferon/ribavirin trial going, but I guess you know that already. It's technically supposed to be for nonresponders, not relapsers, but that's probably going to change soon. Let me get some other information from you, examine you, and get some bloodwork to see if you otherwise fit the protocol. Then we can talk more about what's available."

Dr. Lerner took a detailed history from me, listened to my heart and lungs, and felt my thyroid and my belly. Then he filled out a lab sheet with about a thousand tests checked off and handed it to me.

"You can take this down to the lab. There are a lot of tests, because you have to meet stringent inclusion and exclusion criteria. If you don't, I guess we could talk about trying to get some ribavirin from the pharmaceutical company on a compassionate basis. It takes a while, maybe a couple weeks, to get some of the results back. The viral titers and subtype tests go out to a lab in California. As soon as they're in, we'll call you and set up another appointment."

"Will another liver biopsy be necessary for any of this?" I asked.

"No, you already had two. We'll need to see your slides from those. I can get the one done at HUP, but you'll need to arrange for the one from Cooper to be sent here."

I took the paper and thanked him. I was a little disappointed. I wouldn't know for weeks whether I would receive treatment. I had no choice, though, but to wait it out. I had to be a good patient. Dr. Lerner was my only hope.

Three weeks later, I got a call from Dr. Lerner's secretary, asking me to come in for an appointment. She told me nothing about my labs.

Once more, I sat in a bland waiting room, flipping through outdated magazines. Once more, I was led to an exam room and had my vital signs taken. Finally, Dr. Lerner came in.

"Well, it looks like you might qualify for an arm of the study," he told me. "I can include relapsers, and you'd definitely get both the interferon and ribavirin, because this part of the study looks at the two drugs versus interferon, ribavirin, and ketoprofen."

Ketoprofen is an anti-inflammatory drug usually used for arthritis. I'd heard that there was interest in whether it might decrease liver inflammation. "So you might get all three. But there's one problem."

I suddenly realized that the whole time he'd been talking, I'd been holding my breath. I exhaled. I knew there'd be some snag. It would be too easy if he just signed me up.

"Okay, what's the problem?" I asked.

"You have a positive ANA."

ANA (antinuclear antibody) is an antibody that can indicate autoimmune disease but is often a nonspecific lab abnormality, associated with various other, often benign, conditions.

"Autoimmune disease is a contraindication to treatment," he continued.

"I don't, as far as I know, have an autoimmune disease. I've had a high ANA for a long time, and my workup for autoimmune problems was negative. I've seen a rheumatologist. Would a letter from her help?"

"It can't hurt. Why don't you go see her and get a current

workup, and ask her to write a letter. Then I can take it to the clinical director of the study and ask if you can be accepted."

Another hoop to jump through. And still no guarantee of treatment. I gathered my belongings and headed for work.

A week later, I sat in yet another exam room, this time in the office of Dr. Sharon Strong, a rheumatologist and old friend from my residency days. Sharon sat poring through the reams of tests and notes and biopsy reports I had brought to her.

"Okay, so you have this positive ANA. And you have an old history of some kind of inflammatory arthritis when you were sixteen, but nothing to suggest autoimmune disease now. I think the reason your ANA is so high is the hepatitis. So you might not be treated for the hepatitis because of something the hepatitis is causing. That's a fine kettle of fish!"

I sighed. "I know, it's pretty ironic. But if you can rule out autoimmune disease to the satisfaction of the researchers running the study, I might still get treated."

"Okay, you know the drill. A bunch more blood tests. If they all come out okay, then I'll write a letter saying I think the ANA is from the hepatitis."

"Thanks, Sharon." It was a relief to be with someone I could talk to, and who "got it" without a lot of confusing signals.

Two weeks later, the letter saying I did not have autoimmune disease was on Dr. Lerner's desk. I knew this because I called and harassed his secretary until she made sure it was there, in front of him. I waited a few days and left a message for him to call me. I knew from my own practice that persistence might pay off, but it had to be done right; I was in no position to risk annoying the people I needed help from or they might try to avoid me.

Fortunately, Dr. Lerner returned my call fairly promptly.

"Roz, I got Sharon's letter and all the lab data. I faxed it all to the clinical director for the study, and I'm just waiting for him to get back to me. I should know by tomorrow."

"Who's the clinical director? Is he a hepatologist?" I asked. I wanted to know whether he would understand all the nuances of the medical information.

"Actually, it's someone you know. Dr. Payne—he went to work for the drug company when he left the university."

I almost choked. *Dr. Payne.* What if he remembered me? I couldn't believe it all came down to the same person again determining my fate!

"Does Dr. Payne know whose lab data it is? Is my name attached, or is it all blind?" I asked.

"It's all by number. Not that I think it would matter to him, but he doesn't get any names."

I breathed a sigh of relief.

I got a call from Dr. Lerner's office the next day.

"Dr. Lerner would like you to make an appointment to come in. You've been accepted as a study subject, and he wants to get you started."

I happily made an appointment.

I arrived early for my visit at Dr. Lerner's office. I was greeted by one of the receptionists, who told me I would be filling out some forms, then meeting with Dr. Lerner's research nurse, who would review the protocol with me and give me medications and instructions. The first page in the pile of papers I was given was a description of the protocol. It was highly structured and had strict inclusion and exclusion criteria. I began with the pile of forms. Demographic information, then some medical history, and a list of my medications and previous treatment. Next, an inventory of symptoms. Am I fatigued? Jaundiced? Depressed? Losing weight? Suicidal? Having memory problems? Headaches? And so on...As I rated my irritability on a scale of one to ten and listed the dates and results of my most recent blood tests, I felt strangely calm. Maybe it was the mindless comfort of filling in the blanks, but it was a feeling I hadn't experienced in a long, long time. It resembled hope.

"Dr. Kaplan?" a soft female voice asked. I looked up to see a tall, thin woman with sparkling brown eyes and long, feathery brown hair. She was wearing high heels and a red wrap-style dress under her white lab coat.

"Roz," I told her.

"I'm Barbara, Dr. Lerner's research nurse. You'll be meeting with me for a while today," she said.

I followed Barbara to one of the exam rooms. Her heels clicked out a cheerful cadence on the tile floor in the hallway. She exuded such a positive energy that I liked her immediately.

We sat in the exam room reviewing my forms. She explained the protocol.

"This protocol is for patients who have previously failed interferon therapy. Everyone in the study will get both interferon and ribavirin. Half the subjects will also receive ketoprofen, which, as you know, is an anti-inflammatory drug. There is some preliminary evidence that the ketoprofen may help decrease liver inflammation. Since the outcome is measured purely by laboratory data, the study is not double-blinded. So I can tell you, you've been randomized to the ketoprofen group."

I was happy to hear that I would get the most aggressive combination of drugs. I figured I should go for broke. I nodded as Barbara continued. She reviewed the dosing and administration of all the medications. She went over the side effects. Nothing really scared me. Not even the depression. I had a plan this time—I was already on an effective antidepressant, and I was sure it was going to be okay. The fatigue worried me a bit, but I had plans for that, too. I had already hired a full-time nanny/housekeeper, so the house would be clean and the kids fed and bathed and cared for even if I was too tired to do it all myself.

I did have one overwhelming fear that I had spoken of only to Larry. Barbara made me feel safe, so I also told her.

"I'm not afraid of the treatment. I can handle it. I've felt bad before, and I've managed. It's the possibility that it could fail and I could relapse again that scares me. I don't know if I can tolerate another disappointment."

"If it happens, we'll deal with it. There will be something else. That's not what you need to focus on now, since a year is a long time. Besides, I have a good feeling about this. I think it's going to do the trick."

It was just what I needed to hear. For the first time since my diagnosis, I felt safe and cared for. Of course, I knew that Barbara could be wrong. It didn't matter. I believed that she cared.

CHAPTER 14

# Guinea Pig, Take Three

THE FIRST DAY of treatment included 1,000 milligrams of ribavirin, taken orally, and then an interferon injection in the evening. I had been randomized to the arm of the study that also included ketoprofen, an anti-inflammatory drug that I had to take three times a day. Having had the interferon twice before, I was not afraid of the side effects in the short term, though I knew it would be difficult to continue it for an entire year.

I gave myself the injection at around 10 P.M. and lay down to watch TV. I expected to feel tired, and after about an hour, I fell asleep. I woke up soon after with violent, shaking chills. I got up and put a robe over my pajamas, but I continued to shake. I was freezing, despite layers of clothing and blankets. I woke Larry, who must have been alarmed, as he jumped out of bed to help me, which is very out of character for him. He got Tylenol and tea, but after another half-hour, things were no better. He paged Barbara, who called back promptly. Larry spoke with her briefly, then told me the reaction was not unusual. Once the Tylenol kicked in, the shaking calmed and I went to sleep.

When I awoke in the morning, my muscles ached and my head felt foggy, but I had no more chills. I got up and started my day. *I can do this,* I told myself, but I wasn't sure whether I could tolerate the shakes every other day for a year.

Fortunately, it did not recur with subsequent treatments. The second and third injections were uneventful. I noted a dry mouth, presumably from the ribavirin, and felt very tired by the second week, but I was still standing.

After two weeks, I returned to Dr. Lerner's office, where I again filled out a stack of questionnaires on everything from aches and pains to thoughts of suicide. My vital signs were checked and I met with Barbara, who reviewed the side effects and gave me suggestions for making myself more comfortable. She sent me to have my blood drawn to check for anemia, a common side effect of ribavirin. The medication causes red blood cells to break down, and if hemoglobin levels dropped too much, the ribavirin dose had to be decreased. Blood tests for liver function were also drawn; it was very early in the treatment, but early normalization of liver function tests was considered a good sign.

CHART NOTE 4/15/98
Intense rigors following initial injection. No redness or soreness at injection sites. Appetite ok.

A couple of days later, Barbara called me. My blood count had dropped a bit, not enough to decrease the ribavirin dose yet, but it would have to be monitored closely.

But the real news was that my liver function tests had already normalized, a very good prognostic sign! I stifled my urge to jump around and celebrate; I'd been burned before by "good prognostic signs." We'd just have to wait and see.

A month went by. I was dragging, but so far it wasn't so bad. Larry and I were planning to go to Santa Fe for a Wilderness Medical Society conference, and I was looking forward to the change in climate. My in-laws had volunteered to stay with our children, so we'd have a few days of "couple time"; I figured it would perk me up.

I had my blood drawn again, but this time my hemoglobin had dropped much more significantly, down from 12.0 to 9.5. The ribavirin dose would have to be decreased, but Barbara assured me that lower doses seemed to be just as effective. My liver tests were still normal. I would just have to get another hemoglobin level drawn next week.

"I'm going to be away next week, in Santa Fe," I told her.

"You can have the blood drawn there and have the results faxed to me, or just call me when you get the results," Barbara said. "And remember, your interferon has to be refrigerated. You'll need to put it in an insulated bag with ice and bring it with you on the plane. When you get to your hotel, have them refrigerate it for you immediately."

I hadn't thought about all that. The trip was certainly going to present challenges, but they were not insurmountable. I agreed and took my prescriptions.

CHART NOTE 5/7/98

Hgb less than 10. Phone call to patient to decrease Ribavirin dose to 600 mg qday. Follow-up 2 wks.

We arrived in Santa Fe in the evening, after an uneventful flight. I'd worried that I would be questioned about my refrigerated vials and my syringes going through security, but nobody batted an eyelash. The concierge at the hotel was gracious and attentive as I explained about refrigerating my medication and informed him that I would need access to it the following evening. It was so easy that I could almost forget I had a medical problem.

I immediately loved Santa Fe's desert colors, but with those colors came desert aridity. I would never have minded that under ordinary circumstances, but ribavirin causes dry mouth and dry skin, so the first morning there, I made a trip to the pharmacy to stock our hotel room with extra skin lotion and bottles of water. Even with the additional hydration I was still uncomfortable. My insatiable thirst and feeling of dehydration made the dry air feel like an assault.

The Wilderness Medicine Meeting was a series of lectures and workshops, and a variety of outings into the New Mexico desert were offered in the late afternoons for relaxation. Larry and I love hiking and happily signed up for a hike the next afternoon into an area of desert rock formations known as "The Tents." We attended some lectures and had a wonderful Southwestern lunch at a local restaurant. By 2 P.M. I began having horrendous heartburn, which I ultimately attributed to the spicy food. I had never experienced heartburn before in my life, and I suddenly was acutely aware of why so many medications for acid reflux exist. Unfortunately, I had no such medications with me. I bought TUMS in the gift shop at the hotel where the conference was taking place, and consumed the whole package with no relief. By 4 P.M., I decided I'd need something stronger and told Larry I had to leave the conference to go to the pharmacy.

"What for now?" he asked.

"I need some prescription antacid."

"Really? You never have reflux."

"Well, I do now. I really have to go," I told him.

"It's a long walk to the drugstore from here," Larry reminded me. "Do you know how to get there?"

"Not really, but I'll ask for directions."

"I know where it is," he sighed. "I'll go with you."

This was one of those sticky points in our communication. It was obvious that he didn't want to go. But if I called him on not wanting to go, he'd deny it. On the other hand, if I accepted the offer, I'd have to put up with his annoyance at being dragged away from the conference. At this point, I was suffering and didn't care. We trudged to the drugstore in the afternoon heat.

Even the medication I got did not entirely relieve the heartburn. It was hard to find anything to eat that wasn't spicy in Santa Fe, but I at least avoided the truly hot dishes. Back in the hotel room, I pulled out the package insert that had come with the ribavirin. Acid reflux was not on the list of side effects mentioned. (When I got home, I asked Barbara about that. In fact, many patients had been reporting heartburn on the protocol, and she assumed it was the ribavirin, since patients on interferon alone do not complain of it.)

That night, I pulled out the phone book from the bed stand in the hotel room and looked under "Laboratories." I needed to get my blood drawn the next morning. Several outpatient labs were listed. I wrote down the numbers.

I got up early the next morning and began calling the numbers I'd recorded. I got the same answer from each place. They would not honor an out-of-state prescription for blood tests. It had to be from a local doctor. I called the local hospital, hoping their lab would be more reasonable. No, they told me, but I could go to the emergency room and ask the ER doctor to write me a prescription to get my blood drawn.

By this time, Larry was up and itching to get to the conference. I reminded him that we first had a mission to complete. When I explained that I'd have to go through the hospital emergency room, he rolled his eyes.

"I know; I don't want to go through all that either. But I don't seem to have a choice. I'll drop you at the conference and go by myself."

"I don't want you driving around by yourself in a city you don't know. I'm going to go with you," Larry said. "Do you have directions to the hospital?"

"Yeah, right here," I replied, feeling like a burden.

Finding the hospital was no easy task, and getting what I needed was even more difficult. We wasted the better part of the morning negotiating the maze of medical bureaucracy. Larry was irritable about missing so much of the morning program, and I began to feel angry at his irritation.

"You're blaming me for missing the meeting. I told you I'd do this myself! You chose to come and now you're mad at me." I knew I was whining, but I didn't care.

"I'm not mad at you. I'm just frustrated." He had a warning tone in his voice and his jaw was set in annoyance.

I longed to be irresponsible—to ignore my doctor's order to

get my blood drawn, to skip a day of treatment in favor of enjoying a hike in the New Mexico desert without feeling tired and achy. But I'd come this far, and I wasn't going to jeopardize my last hope for treatment. I was going to do it by the book.

Finally, one of the ER physicians picked up my registration form and called me in. I explained the situation. He had never heard of interferon or ribavirin, but he was sympathetic to the situation and gave me a prescription for the blood tests I needed. A short wait in the outpatient lab and we were done. They told me to call after 2:00 for my results.

We caught the end of the morning's lectures and attended a lunchtime workshop on travel vaccination. Then we were off to the desert for our hike. We arrived at the meeting place to find 20 other hikers, several guides, and four llamas, which would climb with us and pack our water and a picnic. We began an ascent into some amazing red rock formations that looked like dozens of teepees in the sky above us.

The city of Santa Fe sits at an altitude of 7,000 feet. Eight thousand feet is the minimum elevation referred to as "high altitude," and generally people get no symptoms of altitude sickness, such as shortness of breath or nausea, at an altitude lower than 9,000 feet. I ordinarily feel the altitude when I get to 10,000 feet, and generally don't feel sick below 12,000. The Tents could not have been more than 1,000 feet above Santa Fe. A strong hiker, I ordinarily would have been fine on a much steeper climb and at a much higher altitude. But that day, I was short of breath. I started the hike at the front of the group, leading a llama named Michael, who sang and spit at me as we walked. After ten minutes, I began to slow and drop back, and I soon asked another hiker to hold Michael's leather lead. I huffed and puffed my way up the trail like a three-pack-a-day smoker.

After a while, I began to feel dizzy and nauseated as well as dyspneic. I thought about sitting down. But all around me, hikers, many of whom were decades older than I, were practically skipping up the trail. Stopping would be too humiliating. Others would ask me if I was all right, and with all these doctors, people would hover and get concerned. Larry would feel obligated to stay with me. Having been through the boot camp of medical training, I felt I had to push ahead. So I kept climbing.

By the time I got to the top—where there was, I had to admit, a spectacular view—the majority of hikers, including my husband, were already headed back down. I sat on a rock, sweat pouring off my face, gasping for breath. A few people asked me if I wanted to head down with them, but I pretended I wanted to sit and look at the view. In fact, I couldn't have gotten up from that rock if I tried.

After a while, I mustered up the energy to hike back down. Everyone was at the bottom of the trail, socializing and eating snacks. Larry asked where I'd been, saying he was starting to worry.

"I'm fine," I told him. "I just wanted to take my time and enjoy the scenery."

Later, back at our hotel, I called the lab for my blood count. My hemoglobin was down below 9. Fewer red blood cells meant less oxygen to the tissues. No wonder I'd had altitude sickness at barely 8,000 feet. I'd have to call Barbara and have my ribavirin dose further decreased.

I took it easier the rest of the trip. My body was giving me a message that I couldn't keep on pushing it. I was going to have to listen.

After the first three months of the study, blood was sent for viral counts. If virus was undetectable at 12 weeks, the prognosis for a long-term remission improved. Visits to Dr. Lerner's office were now only monthly, but each time the questionnaires on physical and psychological symptoms had to be completed.

CHART NOTE 7/1/98

Dr. Kaplan is receiving Interferon at a dose of 3MU and Ribavirin that has been decreased to 600 mg a day due to symptomatic anemia. At present, she is doing well with mild flu-like symptoms and an occasional rash on her hands. Her transaminases have decreased to the normal range. Now, 12 weeks into therapy, we will check a hepatitis C RNA by PCR.

I waited anxiously for the results of my viral count. After two weeks, I could no longer stand the suspense and I called Barbara. I had to wait for her to return the call, and while I waited, my heart pounded and my stomach did flips. I tried to tell myself it was only one of many indicators, and that not much could be made of the result, even if it was good. Yet somehow, I felt this test was terribly important.

The phone rang. Barbara's cheery voice greeted me. "It's undetectable."

"Really? You're sure?"

"Absolutely. I told you, I think this is going to work. Anyway, this is good news. How are you feeling?"

"Fine," I told her. I hadn't really been feeling fine at all, but the moment of good news made me forget my complaints temporarily. "I'll see you in a couple weeks. Thanks."

By the next scheduled visit, the four-month mark, a few new symptoms had cropped up. I had lost my appetite and was losing weight, though I had no gastrointestinal symptoms. I had noticed quite a bit of hair falling out, too. Because my hair was extremely thick, it was not a cosmetic problem, but I had to sweep my white bathroom floor twice a day because of all the dark strands on it. But the strangest thing was that my usually curly, kinky hair was growing in stick straight.

**CHART NOTE 8/18/98**

Decreased appetite, not interested in food. Fatigue. Not exercising. Hair completely straight! (was curly). Weight decreased about 5 lbs.

After this point, the side effects stayed pretty much the same. I plodded along. I was tired every day, but not tired enough to stop working or change my routine. I felt lucky to have Betty, the nanny/housekeeper, to help with the kids and the chores. Without that help, I doubt I could have kept working. I tried to save enough energy to do things with my kids, but I had to say no when I was asked to volunteer at the school book fair or chaperone a field trip.

It really wasn't until the last couple of months of treatment that I really felt the toll it was taking. Around January of 1999, I started feeling as though it was all too much. My medical practice had become very busy and I was on my feet, without much of a break, all day on the days I worked. We were often overbooked, and I had to move through many patient visits very quickly. I frequently had to take charts home at night to finish my notes because I had no time to write between patient visits, so work often extended well into the evening. Even with Betty's help, I still had the "second shift" when I got home.

My children would be fed and bathed, but they needed help with homework, notes signed for school, playdates arranged, and, of course, general attention from Mommy. I found myself feeling overwhelmed and irritable on many days. I didn't feel satisfaction from a positive patient encounter or get excited by a challenging diagnosis, as I always had in the past; I just wanted to finish my work. I didn't want to watch Maddy's impromptu dance performance when I got home, and Max's enthusiastic chatter set my nerves on edge. I just wanted to be left alone.

CHART NOTE 1/20/99
Fatigued and irritable. Tired of treatment. Appetite fair. Forcing fluids.

Barbara was definitely being kind in her note; in fact I remember yelling at the medical assistant because I was kept waiting, and then refusing to have my vital signs taken. It was only Barbara's soothing reassurance that of course I would feel irritable from the treatment, and that everyone understood, that stopped my tantrum.

Even though the end of treatment was only weeks away, I didn't feel encouraged. I felt between a rock and a hard place: I couldn't stand being on treatment anymore, but finishing meant I might have to face another relapse.

By the beginning of February, I sat in my therapist's office debating the merits of a leave of absence from work. The end of treatment was only a month away, but I'd begun to have severe mood swings, and I often found myself in tears for no apparent reason.

"There's nothing wrong with taking some time off. You've worked your whole life, either in school or as a physician. You've worked through this illness. You don't have to keep doing it," she told me.

"I'm not ready to give up. I feel like I should be able to do it. I'm just so tired."

"Well, it's your call. But you're going to have to take it a little easier, and maybe take something for the mood swings if you're going to try to get by."

CHART NOTE 2/17/99
Fatigue and mood swings. On Neurontin for mood swings.
Last dose of Interferon and Ribavirin 3/9/99.

Surely I could manage for one more month, I told myself, without conviction.

# CHAPTER 15

# The Ripple Effect

WHAT HAPPENED TO me as I struggled my way through my illness and treatment did not impact only me. That which affected me reached into my work and my home, reached to my children, but I think most of all reached into my marriage.

A modern marriage with two careers and young children is a balancing act under the best of circumstances. With a chronic illness insinuating itself into the package, the stress level was periodically overwhelming.

Larry and I were always fortunate to have a strong bond of loyalty. There was never any question of love, respect, or fidelity. But in times of adversity, this was not enough. The fabric of our everyday life together was torn. On the surface, the tears were caused by the interruptions of doctor visits and overnight hospital stays. But the true damage was deeper, undetectable to others, and sometimes even to us.

It started, perhaps, with our coping styles. When I am frightened, or worried, or confused, I handle it by talking about the problem until I find a solution. So when faced with an ongoing worry that seems to have no true solution, I obsess and, in effect, beat the dead horse. Larry, on the other hand, tries briefly, though vigorously, to find a solution, but if none is forthcoming, escapes the worry by throwing himself into work, watching sports, and sleeping. So at the beginning, when I needed to review the "what ifs" over and over again, Larry was doing his best to avoid those eventualities. He became impatient with my repetitions, and I took his impatience for a lack of empathy and caring. In fact, his avoidance probably resulted from the fact that he cared so much that it hurt.

Beyond the issue of coping styles was the question of what behaviors demonstrated caring. Again, I think we had different ideas, but we never actually discussed them. For instance, Larry accompanied me to my first liver biopsy but left very shortly after it was over to go to work, since I was not in any discomfort and the anxiety-provoking procedure was over. He didn't offer to pick me up from the hospital the next morning; he went to work. In his mind, I didn't need him to pick me up, since physically I was fine the next morning, and I certainly knew how to take a taxi. I'd never needed him for transportation before, so why would I now? But I felt neglected being left to take a taxi, probably because the whole ordeal made me feel generally vulnerable, not my usual tough, take-charge self, who would have no problem hailing a cab and giving directions. I never directly told Larry that I wanted to be picked up, so he never actually refused to pick me up. I'm not sure what would have happened if we'd actually had that conversation. I suspect he would not have refused to get me but might have felt inconvenienced, and probably wouldn't have understood why I needed him to do it.

Our medical training may have put information at our fingertips, but it also had made us hardheaded. We both prided ourselves on our strength, resourcefulness, and independence. Consequently, it was hard for either of us to ask for outside support from friends and family. I rationalized this by telling myself that our families and friends were too busy to help us anyway. They truly were all busy people, working and raising families, but I know that if we had admitted we needed support or help, some of them would have been there for us. There were times when it would have helped me if some of our friends had known I was struggling, and provided empathy. Other times, when my energy was particularly low, it would have helped if friends and family expected less of me, so I would have had an "out" from social obligations. But neither of us spoke up about it. Part of the reason for this was the need to keep up a front, a façade that all was running smoothly, that we were having the "perfect" life we'd spent so much energy arranging. Maybe the foolishness of being young made it hard for me to know the difference between empathy from others and others feeling sorry for me. Maybe Larry was afraid of losing face with family and colleagues whose respect he'd worked so hard to gain.

Even within the relationship, we didn't like to admit weakness or neediness. So we created a myth that I was indestructible, despite evidence to the contrary. The myth made it taboo for me to ask for help, since that would be an admission that I couldn't handle the demands of life. Similarly, Larry could not offer help or even be solicitous, as that would indicate he felt I couldn't cope.

Secretly, I wanted Larry to take care of me, especially during the periods of treatment, when I became tired and depleted. I was, even without treatment, overextended between my career and my role as primary caretaker of our children and household. Feeling vaguely ill for months at a time pushed that overextension to the breaking point. We didn't ignore that obvious fact, but we skirted the deeper needs. We arranged for more help in the house, made contingency plans for sick children, and arranged our schedules for optimal efficiency. We made a lot of decisions that seemed to matter, but we didn't address the real issue.

Larry, on some level, didn't want to know about those needs. He was in a critical career-building stage and often came home exhausted himself. He was reasonably involved with the kids, showing up for their sports events and dance recitals and taking them to the zoo on weekends, though he left a lot of the decision-making (who to use as a pediatrician, whether we should seek a speech therapist, etc.) to me. If he heard no complaints, he assumed he was fulfilling his duties. He supported any career decisions I made. He also, of course, supported any treatment I needed, but he couldn't go with me to the place where the fear lay. He didn't see the depletion, and he didn't talk to me about how to relieve the pressure, as I prayed he would. Later, he would say that I'd never asked. He was right; we were both responsible.

I certainly played the starring role in the myth. I didn't want to be seen by anyone in the medical community as being "weak."

Respect was partly gained, after all, by appearing in the hospital at all hours of the night and being available at any moment to discuss patient care. Taking days off, especially since I didn't work "full-time" (i.e., I worked fewer than 80 hours a week), didn't look good. So even if I felt really bad, I didn't call in sick. I got a certain pleasure when other docs who knew I was on interferon treatment said things like "it's amazing that you're managing a full schedule on treatment!" And I hated to miss out on social events or disappoint friends, so I never canceled social obligations, even if I was exhausted. I also felt compelled to be "involved" at my children's schools (the value of that turned out to be its own myth), even if it meant pushing myself more. Larry would see me going to work every day, making dates with our friends, and volunteering at school, so of course he assumed I was up to par. If I wasn't, why didn't I slow down?

The myth began to erode our trust in each other. I wanted help I couldn't ask for. Truly, what I wanted was to be mothered. I missed my own mother terribly at these times. But Larry, knowing very little about mothering, couldn't provide that. The resentment I felt when he failed to meet my needs made me shut him out, and in turn, he felt rejected.

Years later, we would return to this area of trauma in the relationship. Once I was no longer ill, we pushed the resentment and feelings of rejection under the rug, but whenever we disagreed, the hostility left over from that time would creep back in. An argument would start to take on a life of its own, no longer being about the topic of disagreement, but instead about our past disappointment in each other. Though the reality of our situation had vastly improved, our hostility built.

Luckily, there were other, more positive facets of our lives and our relationship that held us together: our children, our commitment to our work, and our belief in the possibility of a good partnership. We still loved each other. Eventually, after time buffered our anger a bit, we began to talk about it. We went back to that painful time. I told Larry that I'd felt he had ignored my distress. I told him that it seemed to me he hadn't been concerned for my welfare. And he told me about how he had felt he needed to be stoic, and act normal, and pretend everything was okay, because he'd believed that if he let on that he was worried, I would fall apart. He'd believed that paying too much attention to the disease would somehow magically instill it with more power than it already had.

There were, even during the most discouraging times, moments when we could see each other with more clarity. It was probably those moments that kept us from giving up hope in the relationship. Once during interferon and ribavirin treatment, I had so many bruises on my legs where I usually injected the interferon that I couldn't find a good spot for my injection. Larry suggested I use my arm instead, but I couldn't get the right angle, so he did it for me. He was very gentle and careful not to hurt me, but the interferon burned, and I winced.

"I wish I could take the injections for you," he told me. "I hate it when I see you suffering. I'd do anything if I could take that away."

As I was approaching the end of my year of interferon and ribavirin, I became less able to ignore my exhaustion. I finally stopped doing a lot of the things that were "unnecessary," such as school meetings and exercise, because I couldn't. I became progressively more irritable and frustrated in those last couple of months. About two weeks before I finished the therapy, I should have been feeling some sense of relief, but I was too tired to feel even that. That week, my family was invited to two bar mitzvahs, both of which were for very close friends, and we wanted to show up for both. We could have, if we'd been willing or able to run back and forth between synagogues and parties. But I just couldn't, so we settled for splitting up, and I went to one service, at my friends' synagogue, while Larry went to another with the children, at our own synagogue.

That evening, I briefly attended a party given by the bar mitzvah family from our synagogue, who happened to live next door to us. As I walked in, friends and acquaintances flocked to me.

I was bombarded with concern. "Are you okay? Is there anything we can do to help you? Are you feeling all right?"

"Wait a minute!" I said. "What's going on? I'm fine! Is this because I wasn't at the service this morning?"

"No," said one of my neighbors. "Your husband said a *m'shabeyrach* [a prayer for the healing of the sick] for you in services today. Nobody knew you were sick, so of course it generated concern."

I didn't know how to react. I was embarrassed by the attention, and I was shocked at Larry. He'd been so staunchly stoic about it all—in fact, stoic to the point that I felt he was impinging on my right to get help or empathy from my community. Why had he suddenly let it all out in public? I gave a quick explanation to our friends and went off to find Larry.

"What possessed you to suddenly say a *m'shabeyrach* for me today, after all these years?"

"I don't know; I guess the last weeks have been so hard, and I needed to do it. I want you to be okay. I needed to pray that you won't relapse again. I hope you don't feel like I violated your privacy."

"I don't," I replied. "I don't feel private about it. It makes me know how much you care."

Hepatitis C was a painful learning experience in our relationship, but one that ultimately drew us together and brought us to understand each other's strengths and vulnerabilities. I learned that if I played the martyr, I would pay for it. Larry learned to move out of his denial and to be more demonstrative. We both learned to speak up. It's the secrets that can destroy you.

Illness can be like a glue, bonding people together to fight against it. But it can also tear people apart. Sometimes the stress generated by illness is stronger than the relationship. Sometimes there are not enough resources to help a couple or a family manage and there is no way to recover from the resulting chaos. We started with a fairly strong foundation, and we had support from other people and enough money so that we were not under other severe stress. Fortunately, in our case, we got glue.

Two years ago, I got a terrible case of food poisoning and ended up in the hospital for a couple of days on IV fluids. It was a miserable thing to have, but in a strange way, it was good for my relationship with Larry. It was the first time I'd had more than a cold in a very long time. It was the first time I'd been sick since we really talked about the effect that hepatitis C had on our relationship. We both handled this illness completely differently than our old patterns would have predicted. I relinquished control and admitted I was too sick to function. Larry stepped in and stepped up to the plate.

This time, Larry took care of me just the way I wanted him to. He stayed with me when I was too sick to care for myself at home, and noticed when I couldn't keep enough fluid down to stay hydrated. He talked to the doctor when I couldn't, and negotiated the maze of emergency room and hospital admissions for me. Once I was better, he was a little over-protective for a few days. I appreciated every minute of his attention and time, and I think he knew that. I felt completely safe.

# CHAPTER 16

# Winning the Race

A STRANGE THING HAPPENED after I stopped my medications. At first, I felt just the same—tired and mildly depressed. But in a few days, my head cleared. I felt like getting up in the morning. I could think. I started moving more quickly. After a few more days, I noticed I wasn't tired at night. I was staying up later, until 11:00 or midnight, reading or playing solitaire. Then I started cleaning my house after the kids were asleep—not sweeping and dusting; the housekeeper took care of that. No, this was intense cleaning, emptying of drawers and closets, and rearranging of items, and disposal of outgrown clothing and broken toys. Ten days after the last interferon injection, I found myself cleaning out the spare bedroom closet at 1 A.M. It dawned on me then that my behavior was not normal. Normal people had energy and did things during the day and went to sleep at night.

The problem was, this "abnormal" felt good. The last weeks of medication had been so miserable—weeks during which I could barely get through the days. I hadn't exercised in months. I'd missed social engagements. I'd enjoyed nothing (except sleep). So the hyperactivity felt like a release, or an undoing, of that time.

I knew, though, that it was not safe to allow the burst of energy to continue. There are people in my family who are bipolar. I had studied bipolar illness and had numerous bipolar patients. The manic phase of manic depression is much more dangerous than the depressive phase, if it becomes a full-blown mania. I knew at that time that I was not technically "manic"; what was happening would be referred to as "hypomania." But I didn't know whether it would escalate, so I had to call my psychiatrist and tell her what was happening. She said she assumed it was related to the discontinuation of the medication (again, this side effect had never been documented before, but since these medications have been in wider use, it has become a recognized complication), and she stopped my antidepressant but left me on Neurontin, which is an antiseizure drug that can also be used as a mood stabilizer.

A few days later, I was able to sleep again, and my energy level had decreased to a dull roar. It was still much higher than when on the medication, but no longer hypomanic. In a way, I was disappointed. I would have liked to get all my closets cleaned out. The motivation to do that quickly disappeared.

CHART NOTE 4/18/99

Energy great. Appetite improved. Looks and feels good. Liver function and Hep C quantitative PCR to be drawn today.

For me, the first blood tests after treatment were the final answer. Both times I'd had interferon alone, I relapsed within three or four weeks of stopping the medication. Though there was no promise that normal tests at this point would mean long-term remission, I strongly felt that if they were normal now, they would stay that way. The hep C experts seemed to agree, though they could make no definitive statement. This was the "big test." I had to believe it would be okay. I wouldn't do it over, and there was nothing else to try.

Two days after the blood was drawn, I sat alone in my office in front of the computer. I could log in to the university hospital lab and get my own lab results. The liver function tests would be back, though not the viral PCR. I had to know, and I couldn't wait for Barbara to get around to checking and calling me. I typed in my password.

Kaplan, Rosalind dob 10/6/60
AST 14
ALT 26
Hep C by PCR pending

Normal! I sat staring at the screen. It was hard to believe. I picked up the phone and called Larry. Without the PCR, normal liver function tests were no guarantee, but this had never happened before.

Larry responded with cautious optimism, which brought me back down to earth. Although I was a little disappointed by his lack of enthusiasm, I knew he was right that we needed to wait for the PCR before getting too excited. He didn't want me to set myself up for a fall.

Two weeks passed before the PCR came back. Each day, I

checked the computer for results in the morning. Not finding them, I tried to put the issue in the back of my mind and get on with my day. I checked again each evening before leaving work.

Finally, I logged in one morning, and the screen with my results popped up:

Hepatitis C by quantitative PCR
undetectable viral load

NEGATIVE! It was over. It was almost impossible to believe! I kept the news to myself for an hour or two, just to savor it. Then I picked up the phone and started dialing. Larry first, my father, my best friend...I started my patient visits so late that day that I missed lunch and had to work at double speed, but I didn't care.

Each day for the next few weeks, I woke up in the morning and had to remind myself that this wonderful thing had really happened. I wanted never to take it for granted that I was one of the lucky ones.

The only remaining matter of business was to get Maddy tested. I had waited all this time because I couldn't face the possibility that she was infected with hepatitis C, yet the waiting had also prevented me from putting my fears to rest. Finally, I was ready to know.

Maddy was six years old, far too young to burden with too much information, so we told her a blood test was part of her routine checkup. She was not at all happy about the needle, but she sat still and let the nurse in her pediatrician's office draw the blood.

We needed only an antibody test. If it was negative, it was enough. If positive, it would be confirmed by the PCR. Fortunately, the antibody test took only 48 hours to come back. I felt as if I were holding my breath for that entire time. Then I called the pediatrician's office and held my breath some more while the nurse looked for the result.

"It's negative," she said flatly. She clearly knew nothing about the significance the test held for my family. It didn't matter. I could start breathing again.

WE WERE ON VACATION in Vermont, at the family resort we visit for a week each year. The kids were off playing with other kids their ages. I could hear their happy screeches at a distance. I sat in one of the white Adirondack chairs watching streaky white clouds in a sky so blue that it seemed too close to the ground.

This had been a place of peace for my family for the last five years. We knew many of the other families who came the same week, and the flow of the day here was lazy and predictable. There were no phones and no TVs, and even the radio stations were very limited. There were no errands to run or meals to prepare or chores to do, and the kids had a multitude of supervised activities to keep them happy, so I was free to exercise, read, write, or think as I wished to. It was here that Larry and I have made many important decisions. One year it was the decision that I would change jobs; another, the decision to move from a house we loved on a street we didn't to a neighborhood where we could feel connected. This year, I was thinking to myself, no big decisions had to be made. I was free. I no longer had to live with hep C's threat casting a shadow over my plans. I was going to just live this week one day at a time.

We were lucky with the weather; every day was hot and sunny. I spent most mornings hiking or taking long bike rides, and spent the afternoons on the lake or at the swimming pool. Each evening before dinner we checked the schedule on the bulletin board in the inn for the next day's activities and signed up for any that appealed to us. Toward the end of the week, I noticed an announcement that there would be a mini-triathlon on the last day of our vacation. Anyone who wanted to participate was asked to sign up ahead of time.

The triathlon, I recall, had been held each year. I never really took much notice of it in past years, but for some reason, it caught my attention this time. I read the smaller print.

Half-mile swim in Lake Champlain around the tiny island. That didn't seem so hard. Eight-mile bike trip into town and back. I knew I could do that; I'd been riding twice that distance most days that week. Finally, a mile run around the resort. *I'm not a runner,* I thought; *I don't know if I could do that, but it's only a mile... Wait a minute, what am I thinking? Just a couple of months ago I was at a physical low. How can I possibly expect to finish, never mind win, a race? I've never been in a race in my life. Why would I try to do this now?*

"Do you think I can do that?" I asked Larry.

"Probably," he replied. One thing I've learned about Larry is that he is the eternal optimist.

"I think I might try."

"If you want," he suggested, "I'll do it with you." He was

suddenly attentive, surprised at my interest. Maybe he wanted proof of my recovery, too.

THE DAY APPOINTED FOR the triathlon dawned cool and cloudy. We spent the morning relaxing and reading at the inn. After lunch, we dressed in bathing suits and brought towels, shorts, and bike shoes down to the swimming dock. Our bikes were ready, tires pumped up and gears oiled, helmets hanging from the handlebars, waiting for us to hop on after the swim.

I stuck a toe in the lake. It was freezing cold. For a moment, I wasn't sure I wanted to get in. It is in my nature to finish whatever I start. Maybe it was better not to start if I couldn't finish.

"Swimmers line up in the water along the dock," the referee yelled.

"Let's go," Larry said.

We stepped down the ladder into the icy lake. I took a spot. There were nine of us lined up, holding on to the dock. Seven men, two of whom were sports staff at the resort and looked lean and muscular in their Speedo bathing suits. The other five men were guests, including an athletic septuagenarian. That left only two women, me and Carol, a perky blond who looked to be at least five years younger than I. We all stood shivering in the lake. Then the starting whistle blew and we began to swim away from the dock, headed for the little rocky island we would swim around before heading back to shore.

After a few strokes, I realized this was going to be more difficult than I'd anticipated. Despite being a generally strong swimmer, I was not used to swimming in a lake, and that day the lake was unusually rough due to a cool Canadian wind coming in.

Each time I lifted my head to take a breath, the water would lap up over my face. Within just a couple of minutes, I was gasping for breath. I could get just enough air to keep going, but it wasn't easy. I watched most of the other swimmers pull ahead of me. A few, including Larry, were struggling as I was. I was grateful for the lifeguard rowing along with us in a rowboat. I wasn't going to give up and get pulled into the boat, though. I watched the island slowly getting closer.

As I reached the rocky area around the island, the water seemed particularly rough. I tried to pace myself and swam around the perimeter. Finally, I was facing back toward the dock. I could hear my heart pounding, and my limbs felt heavy with fatigue. I was no longer cold; numb would be a better description. It felt like miles back to the dock. Everyone else was out of the water by the time I got there. I climbed the ladder, gasping and shivering, and grabbed my towel.

Once I caught my breath, I leapt into shorts and pulled on socks and bike shoes. I ran to my bike and put on my helmet. It was starting to drizzle. I headed out the road toward town. At first I felt wobbly, and the cool breeze made my wet bathing suit feel like a coating of frost on my body. But I quickly reached my stride and began to enjoy the feeling of slicing the air as I sped down the road. I am a strong biker, and soon at least a couple of the other racers were in sight ahead of me. The road to town was flat; I passed fields of grazing cattle, old wooden barns, bales of hay wrapped in white plastic that made them appear as giant marshmallows along the side of the road. Right before the grassy little triangle marking the entrance to town, I passed one of the older men. As I swung around the triangle to head back toward the resort, I passed Carol. She had finished the swim quickly and easily, but bicycling was not her sport, and she seemed to be struggling along. She was, however, a good sport, and as I rode past she held up her hand in a victory sign and yelled, "Go, Women!" I signaled back with a raised fist.

My legs were starting to burn as I tried to keep up the pace going back. I hadn't really noticed the slight grade on the way into town, since it was a downward slope in that direction. Now I was feeling it as I pedaled uphill. Four miles to go, and I'd still have to do the mile run. Larry was somewhere way ahead of me on his bike, as were most of the other men. I slowed a little to pace myself.

By this time, I was quite warm from exertion despite the coolness of the air, but it had started to rain in earnest. I worked hard not to think about my uncomfortable wet bathing suit, the water dripping from the ends of my hair under my helmet, or the rain dripping into my shoes, so that each push of the pedals made a squishy slosh. I was close to the resort entrance now. I could see racers dismounting their bikes ahead and starting the run. I could even see a couple of racers finishing the mile loop of the run and heading for the finish line.

A few minutes later, I approached the endpoint of the bike ride. Spectators were lining the road cheering on the racers. Among them were my own children, standing with some friends and screaming, "Come on, Mom, you can do it!" I hadn't realized they had been at all invested in my performance, and I knew at that point that if nothing else, I was going to try to finish for them.

As I reached the dismount point, I was very surprised to see Larry standing there, running shoes on, waiting for me. I jumped off my bike and started changing my shoes.

"What are you doing here?" I panted. "You were way ahead! You could have placed!"

"I wanted to wait for you. I'm making sure you finish."

I wanted to throw my arms around him and cry. But there was no time for that. We had a race to win, and if I beat Carol, who was not yet back from biking, I'd get first place for women, no matter how pathetic my time was. The man I'd passed back in town was pulling in at that point. I tied my running shoes and started toward the mile-long loop.

Unfortunately, I found that my legs did not want to cooperate. They felt like Jell-O, and even walking was difficult, much less running. I hadn't exercised vigorously in at least a year and a half! How was I supposed to suddenly do this now?

Larry saw me hesitating.

"Come on, you can do this. It doesn't matter how slow you go—you just have to finish." He took my hand and tugged gently as he started a slow jog. I followed suit, and soon we were making our way around the loop. Within a few minutes, the man who had been lagging behind me passed us in an effortless jog.

I periodically had to slow to a walk. I had never been a good runner, and I was panting for breath and had a stitch in my side. There were some small hills, which made me feel even worse. Five minutes passed, and Carol loped past, running at quite a good pace. The loop seemed to me to go on forever. If it hadn't been for Larry's gentle prodding, I would have given up and sat down on the side of the path, hoping that someone would come looking for me in some sort of motorized vehicle. We ended up walking as much as we jogged. I think we did a 30-minute mile, but finally we could see the finish line.

"Let's go, Speedy. Give it a last push!" Larry urged. I thought about all the things I'd done that were more difficult than this—med school, residency, childbearing, losing my mother, taking all those toxic drugs, just surviving sometimes—and broke into a run. Larry pulled me across the finish line to the cheers of a few straggling spectators.

I came in last, but I got a trophy for second place in the women's division. My legs hurt for a week. Despite that, I was overjoyed. My kids were proud that Mom had finished the race. But I think Larry and I were the only ones who understood the true significance. I didn't need to beat the other racers. I'd already beaten all the odds.

# CHAPTER 17

# Being the Patient in the White Coat: Privilege and Price

I WAS TELLING PART of the story of my hepatitis C treatment to a nonmedical friend. He stopped me at the point when I was recounting looking up my own lab results in the hospital computer.

"That's what I've always envied," he said. "You doctors can find out your test results as soon as they're available. You just look them up, and *voilà,* there they are. The rest of us mortals have to wait for our doctors to get a report and then get around to calling us. It's torture!"

I'll admit that checking my own labs is only one of many privileges I enjoy as a physician. My MD and the fact that I am on staff at a hospital allow me not just to look at lab results, but also to walk into the emergency room or any floor of the hospital I have privileges as if I have my ID tag clipped to my coat. In fact, I could probably get away with walking into most other hospitals, too, by wearing my white coat and the ID from my own hospital.

I can call a lab, a hospital operator, or a doctor's office just about anywhere and get through the layers of red tape just by saying it's "Dr. Kaplan" and asking to speak to whomever I wish. Receptionists, assistants, and nurses defer to me. They are as pleasant as pie, even the ones who might leave a patient on hold or snap at another caller with no provocation.

For the most part, these privileges are there for the benefit of patients. I am able to look up lab and radiology results on my computer in my office or on the hospital computers so that I can make decisions about patient care. I can walk into the emergency room or a hospital floor to examine a patient or write orders in a chart. I get through quickly on the phones to share information with other physicians who treat my patients.

I was hesitant to use some of these perks for my own benefit when I had hep C, but not others. I wouldn't then, and won't now, call my own doctors' offices and say I am "Dr. Kaplan" to change the staff's behavior toward me or get to my doctors more quickly. But the stuff that didn't directly involve other people—such as looking at my labs—well, why not? Why should I wait if I don't have to?

Though I didn't overtly take liberties in the doctor's office, I unfortunately have to make a confession. I felt entitled to certain special treatment. Even now I do. When I fill out the forms with my name and address, and there is a space for *Mr., Mrs., Ms.,* or *Dr.,* I circle *Dr.* If I am called from the waiting room as "Mrs. Kaplan," I feel insulted. I don't say anything, but there is something about being called by my proper title that matters. I want them—the assistants and nurses—to know. Because I am afraid that if they don't, they will be less pleasant, less respectful. I want my privileges.

Do doctors treat me differently because I'm one of them? Well, not necessarily. And if they do, as I'll soon discuss, it's not always for the best. Still, some are more solicitous and kind, and some spend more time, knowing that they are caring for another physician. I had doctors during my time with hep C, like Dr. Payne, who weren't kind at all, and I had others, like Lennie, who were supremely kind. It's possible that Lennie was especially kind to me because of my connections. He worked with my husband. Was he that nice to his other patients? Was some of his behavior due only to my physician status? There's no way I'll ever know.

Having connections is another way that I was privileged as a physician. I knew people who could help me, or, if they couldn't, knew someone else who could. When I needed a rheumatologist to give clearance for my participation in the interferon/ribavirin study, I called my colleague Sharon. I'm sure I got an appointment sooner than I otherwise would have because of my connection to her. She was invested in helping me because she knew me. Her letter landed on Dr. Lerner's desk quickly—I suspect much more quickly than if I'd been just another patient.

Recently, my primary care doctor retired. It's hard as a primary care doctor myself to find someone I trust and with whom I feel comfortable. I wanted to go to a certain woman who had been a young professor of medicine at Penn when I was a student. I knew her practice was full and that she was not taking new patients, but I had her email address. A quick message to her got me an appointment. Score one for physician privilege. I know all this is not fair. I feel a tiny bit guilty, but only a tiny bit.

As a patient with a serious chronic disease, and specifically hepatitis C, I had many more advantages than the ones I've already mentioned compared to many other patients sharing my diagnosis. My education was a tremendously valuable asset. Hepatitis C is a complex disease. In the early 1990s, everything about it was news, and everything about the treatment of it was experimental. Protocols for treatment and for monitoring the results of treatment were in rapid flux. For someone without extensive medical training, understanding the symptoms and the potential long-term health consequences of the disease would have been hard enough. Making decisions about treatment must have been overwhelming. I had the benefit of complete comprehension, along with the ability to keep abreast of research, look for new protocols, and interpret the results of preliminary studies. I even knew how to become a research subject.

Along with my education came a stable lifestyle. I had a job, a husband, a family, and financial resources. I wasn't living on the streets, using drugs, living in poverty, living in prison, or even living alone, as so many sick patients were, and are. I had access to care and insurance to cover my medication, especially interferon, which was so tremendously expensive. How could a homeless person with hep C, even if given care and medication for free, manage treatment? Interferon has to be refrigerated. It has to be injected under sterile conditions.

Prisoners generally aren't offered treatment. Patients who live alone may have a great deal of difficulty coping if they develop debilitating side effects.

I was lucky not only to have creature comforts and good social supports, but enough money to pay for hired help at home. Certainly, there have been other hep C patients in my situation socially and financially, but I was definitely better off than the average patient with the disease. I was a privileged patient in many senses of the word.

Despite all these advantages, there is a big downside to being a doctor when you need medical care. It's hard to know where to start in talking about this. Let me first give some hard facts about physicians, health, and self-care. Study after study has shown that physicians tend to avoid seeking medical care. Probably close to half of physicians don't even have a primary care doctor, and well over half treat themselves regularly with prescription medications.

While on the whole, doctors tend to be relative healthy when it comes to major illness, we often suffer many minor ailments, and again, studies over the last 50 years consistently show high levels of stress, burnout, depression, and drug and alcohol abuse among medical practitioners. Despite this, we don't take sick leave, or as much vacation time as people in other professions. We work when we are physically and mentally unfit, at times and in conditions when we undoubtedly would have advised our patients to stay home and rest. Particularly in cases of emotional impairment or substance abuse, this is clearly inappropriate behavior; how can people make good health decisions for themselves when not thinking clearly?

I recently saw a physician for a routine physical who had not seen a doctor herself in almost 20 years. She had received no gynecological care, no mammograms, no Pap smears, and no vaccines, except the minimum requirements of her hospital employment, which in fact had not been enforced, leaving her unprotected from tetanus. When I asked her why she had neglected herself so badly, she cited lack of time as the most important factor. Despite this, she had been feeling guilty and worried that something would happen to her, leaving her teenage children with no mother, and finally decided she needed to seek a primary care physician. This scenario was not a shocking one in the world of doctors and self-care.

Still, the perception of lack of time was just that, a perception. We are not so indispensable that we truly cannot take the time for our own health. Unfortunately, though, we are given the message during our education that we must always serve, and must always be compulsive and overly responsible in our work. Taking that time may seem like cheating in some way, particularly to younger doctors.

In my community, another physician lost a battle to colon cancer after ignoring abdominal pain for a prolonged period of time. She had diagnosed herself as having a minor ailment and self-prescribed symptomatic relief. This kind of denial and self-neglect—caring for ourselves in a shoddy way that we would never apply to our patients—is another risk of our profession. We take some pride in being strong and able to handle anything. Presenting to another doctor for care may feel humiliating. Sometimes a doctor may worry about presenting to a colleague for something trivial and looking like a hypochondriac.

When my son was a baby, I used to hold him on my left side against my ribs. As he got heavier, my lower ribs on the left began to ache. There was an exquisitely tender spot in the middle of the achy area. On the one hand, I realized that the pressure against my ribs from carrying a 20-pound child was the logical culprit. But I knew way too much. I decided that I might have a sarcoma, a malignant tumor of the bone, in that spot. I didn't feel a lump there, but still...I went to my doctor. He was kind enough to reassure me without laughing or saying I was catastrophizing. Yet catastrophizing was exactly what I was doing; it's the flip side of denial. We doctors do both. We might think of every disastrous possibility when we have a symptom, or we might pass off a potentially dangerous symptom as "nothing." We're difficult patients.

Sometimes doctors don't trust their own colleagues. Despite knowing how well trained a colleague is, a doctor may trust only himself, and decide not to seek care for that reason. Or he may go and then second-guess the doctor who is supposed to be treating him. And of course there is the issue of role-reversal, of giving in to being a patient and submitting to sitting in the waiting room, putting on a gown, going for tests, and accepting medications or other treatments. It may seem easier to order and check one's own lab tests or to self-medicate for a symptom, but if something goes wrong, we may be sicker, or more frightened, and have no one to turn to.

It takes a special physician to treat another physician properly. I think the best "physician's physician" will discuss the dilemmas of the relationship at the outset and insist that the patient be a patient. The physician must apply treatment as she would apply to any other patient, while being flexible in allowing a reasonable partnership in decision-making. The treating physician must not assume that the physician-patient knows things (such as how to take a medication or what will happen during a test), but may have to adjust the way an explanation is given so as not to appear condescending. For many doctor-patients, it is very difficult to find that person.

It may take a lot for a doctor to trust another doctor to care for her. That may mean secrets are kept. Secrets don't benefit the patient. This may exact yet another price to the physician-patient. For instance, I don't always tell my doctor every worry I have, for fear she'll think I'm crazy. Consequently, I don't always get every bit of reassurance I need. I don't self-medicate much these days, but if I do, I may not mention it to my physician, because I know self-medication is the wrong thing to do. Most doctors do self-medicate from time to time, and I doubt I'm the only one who doesn't tell on myself. It is also well known that physicians don't own up to excessive drinking or use of narcotic or sedative medications, facts their physicians really need to know about them to care for them properly.

Looking back on my own care when I had hepatitis C, many of the pitfalls of being both a doctor and a patient thwarted my care. Many of my relationships with my treating physicians did not have clear boundaries. I didn't get the clear explanations I needed. I wasn't shown how to use my interferon properly in Dr. Payne's study, since someone, either Dr. Payne or the study coordinator, made the assumption that I would know how to inject it.

I catastrophized some symptoms, such as excessive bruising, and then tried to solve the problem myself rather than talking to my providers. I did this partly because of the poor relationship I had with Dr. Payne, but partly because I felt I could "handle it better myself," and partly because I felt I "didn't have the time to deal with it" properly.

I'm naturally a pretty high-strung person, and I share the characteristics of compulsivity and sense of over-responsibility with many of my colleagues. I also have depression, usually well controlled with medication, but interferon increases depression. My baseline high stress level was, I'm sure, not good for my immune function or my health overall. There is quite a bit of literature that supports the notion that depression suppresses the immune system, as well. If the experimental medications were supposed to boost my immune system to rid me of the hepatitis C virus, then perhaps my stress and depression were counteracting some of their efficacy. My life as a physician contributed to the stress I felt throughout my illness. Stress and depression were subjects I did not feel comfortable discussing with my doctors, partly because of the medical culture. I wasn't "supposed" to admit my weaknesses, especially to colleagues.

I also denied, over and over again, how much of a toll the study drugs took on my body. I continued to work and wouldn't cut back my schedule. I felt I had to soldier on because I was so "indispensable"; my patients and my partners needed me. I wouldn't ask for help when I needed it. I even climbed mountains at high altitude when I was anemic! Now I think, *What kind of idiot does that?* I guess it was the kind of idiot I was at the time. I had my reasons then. They just don't make sense now.

CHAPTER 18

# Picking Up Some Pieces

RETURNING FROM VACATION is never easy. There is the unpacking, the laundry, the pile of mail (mostly bills and catalogs), and the multitude of phone messages, all to be coped with in the one day left before day camp starts for the kids and work resumes for us. The return to home was no different than that from other vacations. But my return to work was different this time.

Though practicing medicine can be stressful, I'd never felt that I didn't want to do it anymore. Sure, there had been days I would have liked to stay in bed, and days that office frustrations grated on my nerves and the heaviness of my patients' problems weighed on me enough that I wanted to run away. But I'd always felt privileged to be a physician, honored by the trust placed in me, and challenged by the problems I was given to solve. So it was a surprise when, more than anything, I felt a sense of dread on that morning I was to return to work.

Looking back, it seems to me that the week in Vermont had

provided me the first real meditative time I'd had in nearly a decade. The pace of my life, coupled with the always-present worry about my health, had kept me from reflecting on the substance of my existence. In Vermont I began to examine it from my new perspective.

What I saw when I looked at my work was not a pretty picture. I saw, like a home movie, the shape and texture of my patient care, the constant battle to stay on time, the weighing of the few extra minutes spent with a suffering human being against my "efficiency" and the numbers on the revenue reports the hospital administrators who ran our practice pushed in my face each month. I saw the way I had begun to dread visits with my patients who were more emotionally needy, no matter how much I liked them or wanted to help them, because I knew their visits would be a challenge to staying on time. Being late meant that my next patient would likely be angry or frustrated, and it meant I would likely miss lunch. More than anything, though, I saw that the structure of my day forced me to leave some of my patients feeling alone, feeling that I was not with them in their concerns. And I knew what that might feel like for them; I'd stood so many times in their shoes.

So I went to work with a sense of dread, but did my best to meet needs while sticking to the schedule. It didn't work very well. Over the next weeks, I talked with our office staff about the schedule and pressed them not to overbook. I talked with administrators about changing the length of visits. Neither of these interventions helped; the staff, under pressure from administration, continued to overbook. The administrators showed me the adverse effect that longer visits would have on the practice's revenue and reminded me that, despite our busy pace and rapidly increasing numbers, we still weren't breaking even. This seemed impossible to me, but according to administration, the lag in third-party payments and the deep discounts of HMOs and other managed care plans, along with the high costs of running the practice (including lots of staff to do the HMO referrals and other third-party payer paperwork), were keeping us in the red. My contract was up for renewal in less than a year; I would likely already be taking a pay cut. Did I want to further decrease my revenue?

Clearly I did not, but this put me in a terrible double bind. On the one hand, I attracted many patients to the practice, partly for my reputation of paying attention to both mind and body. I was treating large numbers of eating disorder patients and patients with various stress-related problems in conjunction with therapists and psychiatrists. I had spent time obtaining some training in mind/body issues and tried to apply that knowledge to my work. Yet the time and money pressures I was under demanded that I do a less than optimal job with those patients. I did my best; I saw the need in their faces and sensed their urgency. Some patients waited weeks for an appointment. I couldn't end the visit without addressing their concerns. So I tried—I skipped lunch and rarely took bathroom breaks. And I brought home a pile of charts in the evening, because I couldn't finish all my charts in the office without missing dinner, too. I did all the things I would advise a patient not to do: I worked too hard, slept too little, missed meals, and avoided drinking water because it meant more trips to the bathroom. It wasn't in the best interest of my patients, nor was it in my own best interest to continue this way.

Yet saying no to a renewed contract was an enormous risk. Other positions in existing internal medicine practices looked no better. Medicine in my geographic area was in shambles, the early stage of the overall healthcare crisis, precipitated by huge malpractice insurance premiums and poor reimbursement for services. A different practice would have the additional negatives of unknown colleagues and having to build a new patient base. I would be leaving the patients with whom I already had cultivated a relationship. I had a "restrictive covenant" in my current practice stating that I could not practice anywhere else within a four-mile radius for two years from my time of resignation, so many of my patients would want to find another doctor close to them.

Strangely enough, it was my regional practice administrator who conceived the path I finally followed. He and I had never hit it off. I was offended by his constant references to the bottom line and what seemed to me to be a lack of empathy for the doctors and staff, to say nothing of the patients. I'm sure he found my lack of enthusiasm for his suggestions regarding efficiency and cost-consciousness annoying. I went to his office to inform him of my decision not to renew my contract that July.

"So what are you going to do?" he asked me in the skeptical, challenging tone he seemed to use for all conversation.

"I really don't know," I admitted.

"You're a little young to retire."

"I can't afford to retire. Besides, I like practicing medicine. I just can't do it this way. I can't stand it."

"Well, you spend too much time with each patient. If you'd learn to work faster and you didn't get into all the emotional stuff, you'd be less stressed." He sounded smug.

"It doesn't work for most of my patients. Their problems are complicated. Their emotional health and lifestyles are not separate from their physical health!" As often happened when I talked to this man, my voice began to rise and I could feel my cheeks getting hot.

"If you're going to be doing psychiatry, then you ought to run your practice like a psychiatrist would. Give the patients longer visits, but charge them. You can't spend that amount of time and energy if you're getting paid ten dollars a month for the patient or thirty dollars a visit."

At first, it sounded ridiculous. I wasn't exactly doing psychiatry. Internists didn't practice that way. I'd heard of a couple of doctors in the area who did have patients pay up front, but they were the big names, the doctors who took care of the rich and famous of Philadelphia-area society. I couldn't do that; nobody would come to see me!

"I don't know; it doesn't sound like something I could do. But thanks for the suggestion," I told him. He seemed to want to help me, which struck me as odd. My guard started to come down a little.

"I actually think it might work for you. You have a niche treating eating disorders; it's not something very many people do. You seem to have a following of patients. Otherwise, you might as well stay here."

"What if I did want to start my own practice?" I asked him. "Are you going to hold me to my restrictive covenant?"

"Look, you know I can't just release you from it. We'd have to make some kind of a deal for you to buy back your practice, if you want to take your patients with you. Think about what you want and call me."

I thought about it. I tossed and turned at night thinking about it. I called my attorney, who had a great deal of experience with negotiating doctors' contracts and setting up physician practices. I talked to Larry; I talked to my partners at work; I called other doctors in the area who ran their own practices. The idea of starting my own little practice and doing it my way had tremendous appeal, but it seemed to me a fantasy, an unattainable goal. I had no business experience and no savvy for the financial aspects. I had no idea what I'd even have to do to make it happen. But the attorney didn't think it was unattainable, nor did many of the doctors with whom I discussed the idea. I let the attorney set up a meeting for me with a practice management consultant. Pat appeared at my door on my day off, a tall, middle-aged woman with sparkly blue eyes and an infectious laugh, a checklist in hand.

We sat down in my living room in the fading afternoon light and got to work. "These are the steps you'll need to take to start a practice from scratch," Pat told me. I scanned the list. Licensing: multiple types. Insurance: malpractice, business, disability, health, unemployment. Space. Contractors. Employees. Marketing. Supplies. Equipment. Bank loans. Telephones. Answering service....

"I can't do this!" I exclaimed. "How would I get all that done by myself? Besides, I still haven't been released from the restrictive covenant."

"I think your attorney has that under control," Pat told me. "But you need to be sure this is what you want. How much time do you have before your contract is up? If I know that, I can make a timeline of all the tasks we'd have to accomplish. You aren't going to have to do all of it alone, you know—some of it would be my job. I work by the hour, and I can give you as much time as you need for initial setup, and then phase out."

"Well, it's April already. My contract is up on the last day of June. I'd have to be in business in July. If I'm going to be telling my patients I'm going into practice on my own, I can't leave a gap in care—I'll need to be available immediately."

"That's right," she agreed. "You have to let everyone know that you're serious and that you'll be there, or you'll lose patients in the transition."

"I'm going to lose most of my patients anyway, once they find out I'm not taking their insurance plans," I reminded her.

She seemed undaunted. "Look, you're taking a risk, but it sounds like you were so unhappy before that you need to do it. From what I hear, you have enough of a niche and enough of a following to make it work. We'll just have to keep the budget low."

As I became more and more convinced that it was the right thing to do, I let myself start to feel excited at the prospect.

"Do we have enough time to pull it off?" I asked.

"It will be tight, but I think it can be done."

That night, my attorney called to say he had a deal to present to me. I would be allowed to work within the four-mile radius and could have my patients' charts as I needed them. I could write a letter to my patients outlining my plans as long as the letter made clear that I was leaving the old practice so as to "concentrate on eating disorders and other psychosomatic issues." The old practice would send out a letter letting patients know where I could be found. They had reached an agreement on a reasonable sum of money for me to pay them in return.

The price turned out to be quite a bit less than I'd expected. So we were off and running; I was going into practice.

Space was the biggest issue. I wanted to stay close to the hospital where I admitted. Unfortunately, space was hard to find there, as well as being very expensive. But through talking to everyone I knew in the area, I was offered a space in a small, older building right across the street from the hospital. It was comfortable and homey, with pink carpeting in the waiting area and high ceilings. One of my two rooms would be my consultation room and contain my desk; the other would be outfitted with a sink, counter, and cabinets, to be used as an exam room. I would be sharing the building with a group of psychotherapists involved in eating disorder work. It was *b'shert* (Hebrew for "ordained"), a match made in heaven.

Pat helped me through the piles of government and insurance company paperwork. I was quickly approved for malpractice insurance, and Pat submitted the other applications and forms.

The next big challenge would be to find someone to act as both receptionist and medical assistant to me. Pat put an ad in the local papers and began collecting résumés.

Meanwhile, I continued to work in the group practice each day. It was May, too early to announce that I was leaving to patients or staff, so I chugged along—seeing patients, rounding in the hospital, writing in charts—while I arranged my new practice in my "spare time."

On a day that was particularly overbooked, I ran even farther behind than usual because the medical assistant who usually helped me was out sick, leaving me with a temp named Summer who couldn't even file charts correctly, much less take accurate vital signs. I walked into an exam room to find an exasperated patient waiting for her physical exam.

"I'm so sorry to have kept you waiting," I began…

"I'm sorry, too," she said sardonically. "You know, I have time constraints, too. I took time off from work to come here. I had a ten-thirty appointment and now it's nearly eleven-thirty! I understand that I might have to wait for a few minutes, but this is way too long!"

"I really am sorry," I told her. My chin was trembling; I tried to keep the tremor out of my voice. "I understand you also have time constraints. I can try to work as efficiently as possible with you now or, if you prefer, we can reschedule."

"Why, so I can wait another hour next week? No way."

"Okay, then let's get going," I said.

I sat down to review her history. The rest of the visit went smoothly, but the patient was still rather put out when she left.

I looked up at the clock in the hallway. Twelve-fifteen and still five patients to see before the afternoon session, which started at 1:00. Obviously, no time for lunch. I also needed to go to the bathroom but someone was in the staff restroom, and I didn't have time to wait.

"Doctor, your next two patients are ready," said Summer.

"Thanks."

I picked up the chart from the first door and glanced at it: a 31-year-old man with a bad cough. This should be a simple one. I swung the door open, and there sat an elderly woman with a cane.

"Oh—I must have the wrong chart!" I exclaimed. "I'll be right back."

I found Summer and told her the problem.

"Oh," she said vaguely, "This man's in room four. I must have put the wrong chart on the door. But I don't know who the woman is—there's a man's chart on the other door, too."

I tried to be patient, though I wanted to explode. "I will go see this man, and you please go ask that woman her name and then find her chart! And you'd better see if this other man whose chart is on the door is in the waiting room or what!"

"Well, you don't have to get snippy at me," she sniffed. "How am I supposed to know? I'm a temp!"

I was about to tell her I wasn't being snippy and that being a temp wasn't a good excuse for not knowing a young man from an old woman. But I realized the futility, and just mumbled "Sorry" as I walked into my office and sat down at my desk. I put my head in my hands. *This too shall pass,* as my mother would say.

"Can I help you, ma'am?" a voice said.

I looked up. "What?" I asked, incredulous.

"Is there something I can do to help you, ma'am?" asked a chunky blond woman in a nurse's uniform.

"Who are you?" I asked.

"Lori. I'm the temp they hired to do phone triage, but I saw you could use some help, so I figured it would be okay to come back here and help you between phone calls."

"How long have you been working here?" I asked.

"A few days—you know that other girl up front, Sharon, is on leave of some sort."

"Are you a medical assistant?"

"No," she replied, "an LPN [licensed practical nurse]."

"Well, I definitely could use some help. Can you find the chart of the patient in room five and then set up room six for a pelvic exam? I'm not sure if Summer is ever coming out of the chart stacks, or if I even want her to."

"Certainly, ma'am."

"And Lori, you don't have to call me 'ma'am.' 'Roz' or 'Dr. Kaplan' would be fine."

"I can't help it," she told me. "I was a military nurse. I've always said 'ma'am' and 'sir.'"

"Okay, then, if that's what you're comfortable with."

Lori hurried off to get my chart. A few minutes later, she had the charts straight, the rooms cleaned and set up, and was waiting to assist me with the Pap smear I needed to perform.

"I hope you don't mind—I told the office manager that you needed more help, so she switched me to be your assistant and put Summer in the file room. She's moving Arlene to the phones, and doing Arlene's work herself," Lori reported.

Too good to be true. The rest of the afternoon was, comparatively, a breeze.

"Lori," I asked her at the end of the day, "are you interested in a permanent job?"

I took Lori's acceptance of my job offer to be a sign. Someone was looking out for me, making sure my plans became viable. The feeling of success gave me enough energy to stay up late each night, making brochures for my new practice on the computer, writing letters to my patients and colleagues announcing my new practice, and explaining why people should pay out of pocket to see me instead of using their insurance card to see someone else. I set up a phone line with an answering machine to take calls from people wishing to get further information or to make appointments.

To my amazement, by the middle of June, my appointment book for July was more than half full. Against the advice of Pat, the office management consultant, I went to Vermont for our annual family resort week the last week of June. It was a lucky place for me; I needed that week so I could start fresh when I got back. I had already packed up all my books and other possessions at the group practice and moved them to the new site. I spent a moment or two looking around at my old office, feeling a pang of nostalgia, maybe even regret. Then I turned and walked out the door, without so much as a glance back.

JULY 1. I AM standing in the pink-carpeted entranceway of my new workplace. Lori is behind the reception desk unpacking office supplies. The phone company technician is hooking up our three business lines. A workman stands in the driveway, hammering a sign saying "Rosalind Kaplan, M.D., Internal Medicine" onto a post on the lawn. A delivery truck sits in front and my exam table is being unloaded. I feel outside of myself, as if I were watching a movie. There seems very little chance that it is all real. I try to concentrate and sound like I'm in charge, but the giddiness in my voice gives me away.

"That's going over here, on a diagonal," I tell the delivery man, gesturing at the exam table. "The EKG machine can go next to the door."

A few months later, Pat and I sit in the building's conference room over lunch. We are reviewing the logistical and financial results of the first quarter of my solo practice.

"I'd like to find someone to share call with more regularly," I tell her. "I'm exchanging vacation coverage with another solo doc, but otherwise I've been covering for myself every night and weekend. So I'm looking into that. I'm keeping up with my bills and loan payments, and even paying myself a little, so I guess that part's working okay. I'm really busy some days, and other days are a little too quiet, but I see the practice building."

"I have to admit," Pat says, "I was pretty worried, especially when you insisted on going off on vacation that last week before you opened. But the fact that you're already on your feet financially is fantastic! It's better than I ever expected."

"I guess I didn't know what to expect," I admit. "I still feel like I'm flying by the seat of my pants, but I'm happy. I'm doing medicine how I think it should be done. Even if I have to keep taking call for myself twenty-four/seven, it's better than it was in the old setup."

A year and a half later, I was "established," ready for a real office space of my own. One of my beloved partners from the group practice came to practice with me. Lori, a free spirit by nature, moved on, but we acquired new staff. After ordering the medical equipment we needed for the expanded office, we looked at seating for our consultation areas. I wanted seating for my patients that wasn't just utilitarian. It needed to be comfortable and beautiful, and to provide a feeling of safety, of encompassment. It needed to provide closeness between patients and their support person, in the cases where they brought someone with them—a parent or spouse, or child, or friend. I looked for a long time, and nothing seemed quite right, until I saw the burgundy couch. It was just big enough to fit two people comfortably, but one person could sit on it without feeling too small or lonely. It was comfortable to sit on, but a person wouldn't sink so deep in it that it would be difficult to rise. The material was a soft, suede-like microfiber, the color of a good merlot. It was perfect.

I doubt I would have taken that leap into my own practice if I hadn't gotten sick, at least not that soon in my career. There's a good chance I would have stuck out another few years in that hospital-run practice, trying to work faster and see more patients in less time. After being the patient who needed the extra few minutes from the doctor, the one who needed a doctor who wasn't burnt out and jaded, though, I couldn't. It wasn't enough to just "do my job" anymore. I had to take a chance at doing it the way I thought it should be done.

# CHAPTER 19

# I See Myself in You

A LITTLE MORE THAN a year after I completed the interferon/ribavirin protocol, I diagnosed a new patient with hepatitis C. Valerie was a single mom, about 30, who came to see me for a routine physical exam and mentioned that she'd been extraordinarily fatigued over the last couple of years. In taking a thorough history, I also learned she'd briefly experimented with intravenous drug use when she was in her late teens and had shared needles with several other drug users. This led me to test her for HIV, hepatitis B, and hepatitis C.

At our second visit, we sat in my consultation room together to discuss results, rather than in an exam room. I told her of her negative HIV and hepatitis B tests, then delivered the news of her positive hepatitis C PCR test and her abnormal liver function tests, definitive evidence of chronic hepatitis C infection. I slowly explained what the numbers meant and what we did not yet know. Halfway through, she stood up to pace a bit. I finished and waited for her reaction.

THE PATIENT IN THE WHITE COAT

Valerie flung herself onto the burgundy love seat in my consultation room, her lip trembling.

"I can't believe this," she said.

I studied her face. She was pretty in an earthy way—wavy
dark hair to her shoulders, a loose dress, sandals. She was
flushed with agitation as she went on.

"This is just what I was afraid of, only maybe worse. I
thought about it as soon as you told me there was something
wrong with my liver. But then I put it out of my mind, because I
didn't think it would really happen!"

"It's not a death sentence," I began.

"It's not good," she retorted, before I could go on.

"No, it's not good. But we don't fully know what it means
yet. And there are treatments available. We need to take this
one step at a time," I told her, all the while knowing that she
wouldn't be able to follow this advice yet, but hoping she would
store it for later.

"Oh, I've heard about the treatment. My friend's husband
got that stuff you inject, and he spent a year lying on the sofa.
He still has it, anyway." She seemed to be shrinking into the
cushioned arm. Her cheeks were wet. I handed the tissue box to
her. She wouldn't hear much of what I said right now; my words
would need to be chosen carefully for maximum impact.

I went on, hoping she'd absorb some of it. "Not everyone
responds to treatment that way. And anyway, you have a ways
to go before anyone is going to prescribe injections. You'll need
to see a specialist, get more bloodwork, and probably have
a biopsy."

"How am I supposed to handle this? I have kids! I have to

work! I can barely do what I have to in a day now. What if I get really sick? There's nobody else to take care of them." Her voice rose so she was almost yelling. Then she got quieter and looked downward. "The worst thing is how I got this."

"There's nothing easy about this," I said, "and it doesn't matter where an infection comes from. It's the same infection no matter how you get it."

I was in my own head for a moment, feeling the need to tell this patient information I discuss only with those people closest to me. I shifted in my seat, trying to decide. *Do I say it? And if I do, will she feel less desolate? Or will she withdraw further? Do I want to tell her because it will help her, or because it will help me?*

In a flash I was back, focused on her face, its shadows, the late afternoon light filtering through the window and illuminating her cheekbone. I was going to do it. I tried to read my patient's expression. She had a blank look, as though she'd gone somewhere else to search for solid ground. I took a deep breath and began to speak.

"I know about what you're going through. Not just as a doctor. I've had it, too. I was diagnosed in 1990." I paused and took a breath. I looked at her. She was bolt upright in her seat, eyes wide. I wasn't sure yet what this meant, so I went on.

"I went through treatment. I can tell you a lot about it. And as you can see, I'm still here and I'm okay. Ask me whatever you want to know."

She was definitely with me then. She was sitting in her seat, back straight but relaxed, and her tears were gone. I felt the tension leave my own body. I'd made the right decision to tell her.

My choice to talk about my experience with hepatitis C with my patient was a complicated one. The unwritten rules of mainstream medicine made self-disclosure taboo, and my formal medical education had urged "professional distance." I was taught that I was supposed to appear invulnerable to my patients, and I was aware of a chorus of voices telling me that patients would wonder whether I would be there for them if I could get sick, and that they would wonder how I got sick, and whether they could contract the illness from me. Especially hepatitis C, a disease that my "doctor-self" knew should carry no particular stigma, but of which my "patient-self" suffered the stigma. Yet I so clearly remembered my own anguish and isolation and despair in the wake of my diagnosis. If only someone who had already navigated the waters had been available to me, perhaps I would have suffered less. And wasn't my job as her doctor to alleviate suffering in whatever way I could?

It wasn't that I'd never told a patient before. In fact, I had told Marie, my eating disorder patient who had been so worried about my weight loss when I was on the interferon/ribavirin protocol. The difference was that Marie had asked, and already had the idea that something worse, something immediately life-threatening, was wrong with me. In that case, an honest answer was the best way to handle her fear. This time, I was volunteering information, unsolicited. I was making this decision, and I needed to be sure my motives were good ones. Overwhelmingly, I think they were.

I referred Valerie to a hepatologist. As expected, a biopsy was recommended. I remember many phone calls from Valerie in the first few weeks after her diagnosis. Fortunately, she was quite comfortable with her hepatologist and was able to ask him most of the questions that came to her mind. Her biopsy showed moderate inflammation and very early scarring. Clearly, treatment was in order. By then, the experimental protocol I got was no longer experimental. It had become the standard of care, and nearly 50 percent of those completing it achieved remission.

Valerie got going on treatment, and it proceeded smoothly. I didn't see her during her treatment; she saw her hepatologist every month and he sent me reports. But when she became worried and felt that he might find a question foolish or "neurotic," she called me. And when she needed reassurance before her biopsy and before her first injection, she called me. I was honored that she did. There was more to it than that. I felt so lucky to be in remission that I felt I owed something to those still living with the disease, and this felt like an opportunity for me to provide it. It's hard to explain. It wasn't a sense of guilt, or that I didn't deserve the remission. I just felt that I wanted someone else to have it, too.

Fifteen months after her diagnosis, Valerie sat across from me in my consult room, on the same burgundy sofa. She was a little thinner, a little paler. Her dark hair was pulled back from her face in a ponytail. The waves were gone. It was the middle of a Monday afternoon, the time of day that the noise dies down in the office. We just sat in the quiet for a moment or two before she began.

"So I'm here because I finished the interferon and ribavirin protocol six weeks ago, and I found out last week that I've relapsed." Her face bore a neutral expression, hiding what I knew were not neutral feelings.

I let the full weight of what she had told me sink in before I said anything. I remembered the feeling of having the wind knocked out of me when I'd gotten the same news years before.

"I'm sorry," I told her. "I know how much you wanted it to work. What do you think you'll do now?"

"Well, my hepatologist is considering doing it again, but I'm not sure I want to go through the same thing again. I doubt it will work if it didn't work the first time."

"Seems like you need some recovery time anyway," I remarked.

"Definitely. Then I think maybe I should just wait until something new becomes available," she went on.

"There would be nothing wrong with waiting," I reminded her. "You know how slowly this disease usually progresses."

"But what if nothing better comes along? I don't feel as though I could live with knowing the disease is just there, eating away at my liver, and not doing anything about it."

"Yeah, I know," I replied, "But you will if you have to. The alternatives are to die, or not to really live, and what a waste that would be."

"Sometimes I wish the diagnosis had never been made," she said.

"Ignorance might be bliss in this case, but that's not what happened." It was not hard to see her point.

After Valerie left, I couldn't keep my mind off our conversation. I was upset by her treatment failure, in part because of my strong identification with her—I kept remembering how devastated I was by my own relapses—but there was something else that I couldn't quite put my finger on. Guilt, perhaps, that the protocol worked for me but not for her? No, not really guilt, more a sort of anger, a sense of the unfairness, the arbitrary nature of the disease—that Valerie and I could have the same illness and get the same treatment, but come out with different results. And I had nothing else to offer her except the lame hope that "something else" might come along. I knew full well how small a consolation that was.

Fortunately, Valerie didn't have long to wait. The very next year, 2001, pegylated interferon, a significant treatment improvement, became available. Valerie, like me, had kept abreast of the literature, and she called me to ask about it before I had the chance to call her.

"I read about it in a support group e-journal and called my hepatologist right away," she told me. "I think I want to be treated again. Do you think it's too soon?"

"Not if you don't. If you can get your support systems in place, I think you can handle it. You're still on antidepressants, right?" I asked.

"Yeah, I stayed on them after the last round. My mother says she'll help with the kids and I didn't take much time off from work last year, so I can take some vacation time if I need it, or cut back hours if I really have to."

"Does your hepatologist think it's the right thing to do?"

"Yes. He wants me to get treated again, and he thinks I have a better shot with this," Valerie said. "I just don't want to get my hopes too high...."

"Go for it, then. And you have to believe it's going to work— why else would you do it?"

Valerie's year on pegylated interferon and ribavirin was

not easy. She told me it was better than regular alpha inter-feron—easier to take, and with fewer side effects—but it was still interferon, and another round so soon after the first was exhausting for her. She had to take six weeks off from work at the end of the course, when the fatigue and malaise over-whelmed her.

She held her breath after the final dose, and prayed that this time she wouldn't relapse. The hepatologist called her with her PCR report eight weeks after the end of treatment: Negative.

I was honored to be the first person Valerie called after her mother. I felt deeply relieved to hear that her ordeal was over. Of course, we'd be checking labs for a long time to come, but I knew it would be okay. Since Valerie, I routinely share informa-tion about my diagnosis and treatment with patients if I feel it will help them.

# CHAPTER 20

# 2004: Here but for the Grace of God

I N THE POPULAR 1991 move *The Doctor*, William Hurt played a talented ear, nose, and throat surgeon with a brash bedside manner who is transformed into a compassionate healer through his own cancer treatment.

Some medical schools have experimented with a curriculum in which students must participate in simulated illness, submitting to the humiliations of multiple physical exams, wearing hospital gowns, and being pushed about the hospital on gurneys.

I don't know if being sick made me a better doctor. I do know it changed my perspective in many ways. I found myself continually surprised in the years I spent battling hepatitis C: finding that some of my doctors were great comforts to me, while others, however unintentionally, served to bruise me; that my patients were often deeply healing, as were certain friends, neighbors, and even total strangers, while those closest to me—often because of their caring itself—backed away when I needed them most. I learned that I did not always feel or behave as I expected myself to, and that the emotional impact of illness was, for me, in the short run, much more devastating than the physical.

As for hepatitis C, I've seen a lot happen over the years since I finished treatment, for better or worse. The disease has become more and more a part of our medical and psychosocial landscape. Maybe I just notice it more because of my experience with it, but sometimes it seems to be everywhere.

Watching the TV news a couple of years ago, I heard that a man with chronic hepatitis C was being accused of attempted murder. It seems he spit on another man during an argument. I wondered briefly whether this could really be happening in the 21st century, but reminded myself that the era of discrimination against AIDS and other infectious patients is far from over; the war on ignorance just took a backseat when 9/11 and the Iraq war took the forefront.

There are news reports and medical reports regarding hepatitis C in the nation's prisons; it has become a serious epidemic, and the prison system now must deal with the burden of illness in prisoners. If treatment is recommended for the majority of patients with chronic hepatitis C, should prisoners with hepatitis C be treated? Who will pay for such expensive treatment? How can the spread of disease be prevented in the prisons when we know that prisoners are exposed to each other's blood through illicit drug use, sex, and violence?

One of my patients calls. Her daughter is being treated for

hepatitis C in another city. She has researched the side effects of treatment, and it is obvious to her that her daughter is depressed. Yet the doctor who prescribes her daughter's interferon and ribavirin refuses to prescribe an antidepressant and her daughter has no mental health insurance coverage. What can she do? I suggest she call her primary care doctor to ask for antidepressants, but I let her know I am willing to see her daughter, at no fee, if it doesn't work out. It is something very small I can do to help someone who is sitting where I sat a while ago. Why should she suffer unnecessarily?

I take a phone call from a friend and colleague between patients. Her nephew, she tells me, is a surgical resident in New England. Three months ago he sustained an accidental needle stick while suturing a patient. He just found out he became infected with hepatitis C from the injury. He is distraught, beside himself. His family, who have not seen him cry in a decade, say he has been tearful and has told them he will never get married or have children, and that he may need to change career paths. Could I talk with him?

I want to fly to where he is and wrap him in my arms, tell him I know his despair.

In reality, I only talk to him on the phone and give him information, data he can assimilate into his surgeon's mind that will, I hope, dispel the myths. I direct him to the most competent care. I tell him that I know where his mind is taking him and that he needs to stay focused on what is actually happening instead of on the worst-case scenario. I tell him to get help and support for his anxiety and depression. I tell him he can call me anytime.

When we hang up, he has a plan of action and seems to be settled down. He is deeply grateful for this, but I know that I have not driven from his mind the demon images of patients with jaundice and bleeding varices, the same physician's nightmare images that I suffered a decade ago.

I still sometimes wake from nightmares with those images, or wake in the morning forgetting that my ordeal ended years ago. Then I remember, and can hardly believe my good fortune. The illness left no mark on my body, save the tiny scar over my rib where the biopsies were performed. Physically, I am free.

Yet in some ways, the ordeal never ends. Recently Dr. Lerner wrote a letter to a disability insurance company, expressing his opinion that I am in remission and that it is "very unlikely" that hepatitis C will have any impact on my health in the future. It didn't help; I still can't get disability insurance, though I did manage to get a life insurance policy from what my insurance agent referred to as a "very liberal company." From an insurance standpoint, I am still a bad risk.

If I were an insurance evaluator, I guess I would say the same thing. Nobody will use the word "cured" yet when it comes to hepatitis C. My doctor wrote his letter based on the very scant data that exists—a single study of ten patients who were negative for hepatitis C virus six months after treatment with interferon was completed, and remained negative ten years later.

Still, I believe that I am done with it. Maybe I believe this because I need to, so I can proceed with my life, but I don't think that's the whole truth. I actually feel that I am healthy, and that the black cloud has lifted from around me. If other people want to use the word "remission" instead of "cure," I can live with that. I think that in the next few years, there will be enough data about long-term remission that the medical community will begin to talk in terms of cure.

Even in the occasional moment that I allow myself to think it could come back, I don't suffer the thought. We all live each day with a question mark. Every day that I am healthy is a lucky day. I can't worry about when the other shoe will drop. If I did, I wouldn't really be living. I'd just be waiting to die.

I could get in a car accident or find out I have breast cancer at my next mammogram. My child or my husband could become seriously ill. I know I am aging; I see the lines around my eyes and the graying of my hair. Things happen to people all the time, and they will happen to me. Hepatitis C is only one of thousands of perils that I have escaped. But today, just today, I live in a state of grace.

# CHAPTER 21

# 2008: Ten Years Out

M Y HUSBAND AND I sit in the office of Undergraduate Admissions at Wesleyan University, waiting for our son to return from his interview with an admissions officer. The small liberal arts school seems a good match for our intensely intellectual and creative son. Max favors the seminar-style classes, the challenging curriculum, the Division III wrestling team, and the supportive, diverse community.

My son will turn 18 this fall. I will turn 48. He will graduate from high school in the spring. Certainly, this is an important year for our family, but for me, it holds a special significance. This is the year that, according to my first hepatologist, Dr. Payne, I "would probably" live to see.

The way I imagined things then was that I would be attending Max's high school graduation as a dying cirrhosis patient. Maybe his graduation party would also be my farewell party. A melodramatic scene, I admit. But I am still very much alive, extremely healthy, free of hepatitis C, and launching my son into his adulthood. I still have my artistic and preternaturally sensitive 15-year-old daughter to guide through a few more years at home. Then she, too, will leave the nest, and Larry and I will embark on an adventure of our own, discovering our lives as a couple without children at home once again. No, I am definitely not dying.

I recently saw a new gastroenterologist for my vague colitis, not because I was having symptoms, but because I need someone to follow me and treat me if it should become necessary, as it periodically does. I decided it was time to leave Dr. Lerner, whose office is rather far from my home. While Dr. Lerner does practice general gastroenterology, he was always primarily my liver doctor, and it seems I don't need a liver doctor anymore. My new doctor looked through my records.

"You were lucky with the hep C," he remarked.

"Don't I know!"

"You had type Ia, it says here."

"Yes, and I know, it is unusual that I had a remission, especially back then."

"Well," he remarked, "even now, it's only forty-five percent long-term remission for type I. But you're done with it. Now, if a patient is PCR-negative six months after treatment is complete, we pretty much figure it's a cure."

"Cure?"

"Well, yeah…"

"Nobody ever says that!"

"I know, technically nobody says it, but the disease doesn't come back if it's been that long," he told me.

I knew this, but it felt so good, even this many years later, just to hear someone I called "'my doctor'" say it.

I like to think of myself as non-judgmental. But when it comes to hep C, I have very strong opinions. I think I've earned the right to them. I believe in screening and I believe strongly in treatment. There are guidelines for the screening of high-risk patients: anyone who had blood transfusions before 1992, IV drug users, and those with tattoos, for example. Still, many of those patients don't get tested, and lots of people who get notices from the Red Cross after donating blood don't follow up. In addition, people with abnormal liver function tests, even if the abnormalities are mild or if they fluctuate back to normal, should be tested, but many doctors fail to do this.

Current treatment guidelines have changed tremendously since the years when I had hep C. Now if a patient has hepatitis C virus in his blood, abnormal liver tests, and no serious contraindications to treatment (such as a coexisting disease that could be made worse by the medication), treatment is recommended. Standard of care, depending on viral subtype, is 24 to 48 weeks of combined interferon and ribavirin. Exciting new research may add a third drug, telaprevir, to the regimen in the very near future, increasing the rate of long-term remission (but at the price of increased side effects).

Biopsy is helpful but not a prerequisite for treatment in most cases. Yet many eligible patients with hep C are not treated, for a variety of reasons. Insurance may not cover the cost of the standard pegylated interferon and ribavirin regimen.

And most significantly, patients decline treatment because they fear the side effects, or believe that the treatment is worse than the disease. I find myself very frustrated with this way of thinking. Why would someone with access to treatment reject it without even trying it?

I am not saying that everyone with the disease *must* be treated. There are appropriate situations in which the disease is mild enough for watchful waiting, and some patients may choose with their doctors to wait for a more effective regimen, especially with impending new medication. However, these decisions should be a collaboration between doctor and patient based on best care, not on fear, myth, lack of access, or poor doctor-patient communication.

I've been to hep C support group meetings during which I've met people in all phases of illness and treatment. Some have just been diagnosed. Others have already undergone liver transplants. Many are getting interferon and ribavirin, and having widely different responses and side effects at different points during the year of treatment. Invariably, there are one or two people trying to decide whether or not to start treatment, and maybe someone who has decided against it altogether. Even those suffering with unpleasant treatment side effects will turn to those people and say, "Don't you want to get rid of the virus? Don't you even want to try?"

I never spoke at support group meetings unless I was asked to present a topic, but I wanted to. I wanted to ask, "How can you stand knowing that there might be a cure, and that you're not giving yourself that chance?" I felt compelled to behave in a nonjudgmental manner, as I do when I discuss such a decision with a patient. I discussed this exact topic with a patient a couple of years ago. He was diagnosed with hep C a decade ago but has probably had it since the 1970s, when he dabbled in intravenous drugs. He'd had two liver biopsies showing progressive inflammation, and his hepatologist had been urging him to start pegylated interferon and ribavirin. He clearly understood his risk for developing serious liver damage over time. Nevertheless, he said he felt fine, and that he was not willing to take medication that might change that for any length of time. He was taking an herb (milk thistle) that is supposed to decrease liver inflammation but that has no proven benefit for hep C.

I gently reminded him that interferon and ribavirin was his best chance at preserving liver function, and that I agreed with his hepatologist. But of course, I would honor his decision and continue to be his doctor regardless of his choice. That is my job.

I can honor the decision, but I don't have to like it. It will never make sense to me. The medications are toxic, I admit, and have to be taken for up to a year. But the virus is pretty damned toxic, too, and without treatment, it lasts a (possibly shortened) lifetime.

Denial is a healthy defense mechanism to the extent that it helps us function in the face of adversity. When it keeps us from moving forward, it becomes a bad habit. For me, it would have been a luxury with too high a price. There was data, even in the early 1990s, stating that 80 percent of hep C patients would remain healthy with regard to liver function 20 years after diagnosis. Yet I was diagnosed as a 30-year-old mother of an infant. My family was going to need me for a long time, and I was going to need my liver for 40 or 50 or more years. I simply could not afford denial.

I will fight for the patient who wants treatment but can't afford it, and root for the patient who relapses or can't tolerate treatment and is waiting for an improved regimen to come along. I hate hepatitis C. My life has been decidedly better without it.

I often hear aphorisms and trite phrases, presumably meant to make someone feel better when there's been a tragedy or a serious turn of bad luck, or really any kind of human suffering. "Things happen for a reason." Or "God never gives you more than you can handle." Or perhaps "What doesn't kill you makes you stronger." These are just a few of the "comforting" adages that make the rounds, and make me cringe. I can't believe that there is rhyme or reason to the way illness strikes. It's clear to me, witnessing the pain, suffering, and death that I do as a primary care doctor, that each person, and each circumstance, has its own psychological wake. I've seen people gain a new lease on life through suffering, but I've also seen it devastate families and embitter patients. Yet no matter how it changes us, we are clearly changed, and often that change is profound.

I see differences in myself that I believe resulted from my illness experience. I wish I could say that I live every day for the moment, that the little things never bother me. I'm not that virtuous by any means. Still, when lesser concerns come my way—a leak in the roof, a financial glitch, a defiant adolescent—I can sometimes remind myself of my ordeal and put perspective on the current annoyance. More importantly, I have much more patience for those around me. I became so aware of my own quirks, my anxieties and vulnerabilities—in short, the cracks in my armor—when I was ill. I continue to have those cracks; they are just glued together right now. When other people are not at their best, or behave in ways I find immediately inexplicable, I believe there is much more beneath the surface. We never know what is going on behind someone else's closed door, or closed expression. I try to remember that each day when I go out into the world.

I also came to see just how much of the suffering I endured came not from my disease itself but from my notions of sickness and health, society's notions of it, and the medical system's treatment of the disease rather than the human being.

"In the sufferer let me see only the human being," says the oath of Maimonides. This, rather than the Hippocratic oath, is what hangs, framed, above my desk at work. I will never live up to it perfectly, but I will keep trying.

# ACKNOWLEDGMENTS

I OWE A HUGE debt of gratitude to Ellen Szabo, who believed in me and in this story, and convinced me to begin this project. But without Alison Hicks and the talented writers in the Greater Philadelphia Wordshop Studio, the original manuscript for this book would be hidden away in a drawer right now. Their encouragement, incredibly constructive criticism, and enthusiasm gave me the confidence to resurrect my story and continue working on it until it took form.

Many of my friends and colleagues have helped me with their comments and input. Thank you Susan Howard, Robin Goldberg-Glen, and Andrea Shapiro. A special thanks to Dr. David Metz at the University of Pennsylvania School of Medicine for his careful review of my gastroenterological information.

Alex Holzman and others at Temple University Press were exceptionally kind and generous with time and effort spent in reading and critiquing parts of the manuscript. I am very grateful for their interest.

My agent, Jeanne Fredericks, has been an inspiration. Her expertise and equanimity made the process of finding the right home for the book at Kaplan Publishing a smooth experience.

She has shepherded me through every step of the way. I have been lucky to have first Rachel Bergmann and then Kate Lopaze as editors at Kaplan. They showed enthusiasm for the project, and provided perceptive editorial notes, as well as attention to detail. Thanks are also due to Dominique Polfliet and everyone at Kaplan for their kind support.

I can't begin to mention all my dear, wonderful friends and family by name, but you know who you are: you supported me through my illness, you knew all the gory details that are in this book before you read it, and you've continued to stand by me ever since.

I must also mention my patients, who give me a reason for trying to be my best self every day. I thank you for giving me purpose. I constantly learn from you and for that I am forever grateful.

To my husband, Larry, who is the love of my life and has lived every wonderful as well as every harrowing moment with me, thank you a million times for being who you are, for supporting this book, and for being my partner. And to my beautiful, amazing children, thank you for reminding me every day how precious life is.

# INDEX

# ABOUT THE AUTHOR

DR. ROSALIND KAPLAN is a Clinical Associate Professor of Medicine at Temple University Hospital, where she teaches Narrative Medicine to first- and second-year medical students. She writes with the Greater Philadelphia Wordshop (GPWS) and is one of the authors in the recent anthology *Prompted,* a collaboration between *Philadelphia Stories Magazine* and GPWS.

Dr. Kaplan has been a speaker at support group meetings for hepatitis C sufferers. She has also been a facilitator of physician support groups based on a program called Finding Meaning in Medicine. She has been listed as a "top doc" in both *Philadelphia Magazine* and *Main Line Magazine.*